After You, Mr. Wainwright

Lakeland books by
the same author:

CHANGING LAKELAND
MEN OF LAKELAND
LAKELAND DALESFOLK
WILD CUMBRIA
THE LAKE POETS
GRASMERE AND THE WORDSWORTHS
BEATRIX POTTER REMEMBERED
LAKELAND BIRDS (with R W Robson)
LAKELAND MAMMALS (with Peter Delap)
LIFE IN THE LAKE DISTRICT (photographs)

After You, Mr. Wainwright
In the Fell Country of Lakeland

by

W R Mitchell

(Editor of "Cumbria", 1951-1988)

Good walking! And don't forget—
watch where you are putting your feet.
AW, 1965

To succeed, first tell yourself you can do it.
Joss Naylor, having run the Wainwright Round, 1986

Keep writing!
AW to WRM, 1990

CASTLEBERG
1992

Castleberg, 18 Yealand Ave., Giggleswick, Settle, North Yorkshire, BD24 0AY

ISBN: 1 871064 65 1

© W R Mitchell, 1992

Typeset in Century Book and printed by J W Lambert & Sons, Station Road, Settle, North Yorkshire, BD24 9AA

Contents

For

BETTY WAINWRIGHT

Illustrations

Cover Pictures: Front, top—Wainwright with pipe (Collection of Betty Wainwright). Painting—Ennerdale with Goldcrest (Edward Jeffrey, for W R Mitchell's Collection). Back cover—Wainwright with camera (photo: Kenneth Shepherd). Map of Lakeland—Alan G. Hodgkiss.

Foreword

by Bob Swallow

MY fell-walking career has been doubly blessed.

I first came to know A. Wainwright through correspondence, having the temerity to question his recording of the number on the trigonometrical column on Wild Boar Fell, overlooking Mallerstang. For the record—as he was the first to agree—we were both right, the original plaque having been pilfered and subsequently replaced with the next available number.

Later, while frequently visiting Kendal on business, I would call for an early morning "cuppa" and AW put the world of finance to rights. Increasingly finding myself in agreement, I took early retirement, seeking pastures new though not before having run a highly successful promotion, with his blessing, whereby a selection of his drawings of Lakeland fells were "blown up", numbered and individually signed by him.

I can still see him poring over a huge pile of prints, diligently signing each with the same meticulous care which characterised all his work. Needless to say, the ink was green—his hallmark.

I also met Betty, his delightful second wife, as diminutive as he was large. Not enough has been heard of Betty, the power behind the throne, a fact that AW was the first to acknowledge.

During later life, when sadly his sight had deteriorated, he would permit Betty to go fell-walking with me. There was a strict admonishment to "make sure you bring her back safely". Perhaps one day in the not-too-distant future she may be persuaded to write her own story. It will make fascinating reading.

Then I met Bill Mitchell.

The first occasion was at a Women's Institute meeting in our village hall. (No—I'm not in the WI). It was an open meeting back around

1982-3 and probably he was speaking about my other love, the Settle-Carlisle Railway.

At that time, Bill was a forty (plus) a day Woodbine man, which didn't do much for his legs and lungs when struggling up Lakeland mountains. It seemed amazing to me at the time that while his knowledge of the daleheads in both Cumbria and Yorkshire was encyclopaedic, the world above 1,000 feet was comparatively new to him.

At a time of life when many folk are putting their feet up at home, he decided to scale all Wainwright's 214 Lakeland peaks. The cigs have gone. Now it is I who struggle to keep up with him on high ground.

Bill's book is tinged with nostalgia. Sufferers of Wainwrightosis will revel in it.

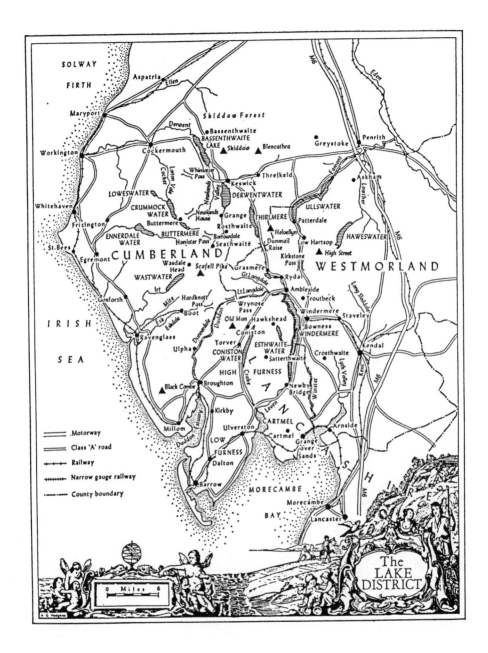

PRE-1974 LAKELAND, WHICH WAINWRIGHT LOVED TO RECALL.

9

Disciples of Wainwright

BOB SWALLOW: Favourite expression—Life is for Living. He really comes alive on a Lakeland fell, with the wind in his face and the comfortable feel of a thermos flask pressing against his back as his rucksack takes the strain.

A Leeds lad, Bob spent many years in Building Society managerial work. After spasmodic correspondence with AW, Bob visited him at his home in 1983 as a prelude to one of his regular business trips to Kendal. Setting off early from home, he usually arrived at AW's home when breakfast had reached the "toast and marmalade" stage and naturally he was invited to have a cup of tea.

With AW's co-operation, he organised a special promotion for his firm which involved a gift of signed Wainwright prints to those who supported a savings scheme. He had previously put to him the idea for a black and white outline of the Lakeland peaks as seen from the stone jetty at Morecambe.

Bob sets the tone of many of our excursions in the Lake District by reading from the appropriate Wainwright book using a Charlton Hestonish voice, which attains its maximum effect in the echo chambers of ravine or corrie and startles the nearest sheep.

He prepares for a fell-going excursion by drinking a gallon of tea. It was Bob who devised the felltop routine of photo-calls and butty-stops. A compulsive photographer, Bob has spent 9.6% of his life in semi-darkness making audio-visual shows.

STAN FIELD: Stan's fell-walking career parallels that of Bob and dates back to their days in Nottinghamshire. His working life has been spent in local government in the North-East and (now) in Cumbria.

Stan occasionally takes a photograph with a camera of such complexity that half a minute elapses before the mechanism calms down. No one has actually seen one of his photographs, but he has a domestic display of landscape paintings. He periodically threatens to paint a portrait of one of his walking friends.

Stan has achieved his ambition to live and work in the Lake District and rejoices after many walks that he is only 20 minutes' drive from having a hot bath.

COLIN POMFRET: Like Bob, he took up employment with a Building Society. Unlike Bob, he still passes his days busily behind a desk, absorbed in talk about mortgages and interest rates.

With a home just north of Southport, Colin manages to cram 25 hours of travel into a "walking" day. He is supremely fit and has been known to run up Lakeland fells and to jog-trot a mile or two at the end of a long walk to collect the car.

He has been keeping his last half dozen Wainwrights unclimbed for ages while wondering what to do next. There must be Life after "doing the Wainwrights" but it can't amount to much.

BILL MITCHELL: The oldest member of the group, Bill incinerated cigarettes by the yard until, on his retirement from work (laughter), and having known AW for years, he had the urge to "do" all the Wainwrights. When his lungs were decarbonised, he joined the trio of walkers on the fells. Having progressed from the "nursery" slopes of Fairfield (immoderate laughter), he bought an ice axe at Bob's insistence. Bill is now saving up for crampons and then he will be a "proper" fell-walker. He ruefully observes that Wainwright bestrode the fells in his ordinary clothes, plus mackintosh and studded boots (whistles of amazement).

Bilberries and Sheep Droppings

(Aspects of Biography)

Wainwright's Chief Likes and Dislikes

LIKES:

Betty
Skylines
Pipe and Tobacco
Fish and Chips
Maps
Well-used Boots
Blackburn Rovers
"Coronation Street"
Old Kendal
Cats (not so keen on dogs)
Yet More Fish and Chips

DISLIKES:

Gaelic Names for Scottish Mountains
Sociable Fell-walkers
Passing the time of day with School Parties
    (one "good morning" had to do!)
Car Seat Belts
Cruelty to Animals
Bad Grammar
Most places South of Blackburn

TO WAINWRIGHT, Lakeland was heaven. The television series *Coronation Street,* with its rich assembly of characters, was a weekly reminder of where that road to heaven had begun—in a Lancashire milltown.

It was an unpromising start. At Blackburn and the other textile towns the hills were revealed only when a forest of chimneys stopped smoking in Wakes Week. And you will have heard that old story about the crows flying backwards to keep the grit out of their eyes.

Wainwright, shy and awkward but most determined to improve his lot, became Britain's best-known hill-walker. His seven pictorial guides to the Lake District, which have sold well over a million copies, are an enduring memorial to his originality of mind and fine penmanship.

This book is not just about AW, as he was known to his close friends. It concerns a small group of admirers who follow in his footsteps. There is space for notes on only a few of the Wainwright fells, which of course are fully dealt with in his famous pictorial guides.

As sufferers of Wainwrightosis, Bob, Stan, Colin and I do not wish to be cured. We do not suffer, except for the frustration of not being able to spend part of every day on the roof of Lakeland. Wainwrightosis loosens our tongues. We are inclined to jabber, drinking in views as well as tepid tea, forever mentioning Wainwright's distinctive way at looking at the finest landscape in England.

A flask of tepid tea was broached when I conquered Dale Head, the half-way point in my own pilgrimage. The three-quarter point was reached on Binsey, a dimple on the Cumbrian landscape near Bassenthwaite.

Our appetites are sharpened by mountain air. In between spells of walking and photography, we are commanded by Bob to sit down for a snack, known as a "butty stop" (which Bob himself will define on a later page).

We have consumed our butties while perched, eagle-like, on ledges above Wasdale, in the broiling heat on Glaramara and within an old croft above Ullswater—a croft that was hastily vacated by a sleepy fox.

The low point came with the consumption of tomato sandwiches in the rain on High Street. Our food has taken on strange shapes, including V-shaped sandwiches, pancake-flat sausage rolls and an amorphous cake/bun confection.

AFTER YOU, MR WAINWRIGHT—the book, that is—really begins with bilberries and sheep currants. Bob Swallow was in the process of compiling a programme of slides and music about Lakeland. He naturally wished to include a reference to AW.

It was late summer. At our chosen tract of ground, on the flanks of Gragareth Fell, we had no difficulty in finding fresh sheep droppings but the red grouse seemed to have consumed the bilberries. After half an hour's quest, we had three, one of them being slightly squashed.

Bob photographed them in ultra-close up. He was making a typical amusing Wainwright point: that it is important for an apprentice fellwalker quickly to learn the difference between bilberries and sheep droppings. The former tend to taste sweeter! We laughed at Wainwright and ourselves. And in next to no time this book of happy memories was devised.

Wainwright was by no means the first Lancashireman to cut loose from the gritty background of mills, pubs, chapels and terraced housing to settle in the Lake District. His inclinations were similar to those of Joseph Hardman, who quit Lancashire milldom for Kendal and for many years joyously explored the Lake District, leaving the area once a year—to have a week's holiday at Blackpool.

Wainwright traversed Lakeland by public transport when compiling his seven pictorial guides. Joe Hardman hired a taxi, taking with him his plate camera, stack of photographic plates, his wife and at times pretty nurses from Kendal hospital who, in return for posing with attractive Lakeland backgrounds, had a day out and were treated to tea.

Wainwright carried a camera in order to prepare meticulous drawings to accompany his miniscule hand-writing. He attempted to draw and write a guide book page a day, being diverted from his mission only by his cats and the television series *Coronation Street*.

What on earth did we do to enlarge our experience of Lakeland in the pre-Wainwright age of guide books? Early works were heavy on prose and light on illustrations. Baddeley and H H Symonds were among my favourites. Heaton Cooper provided meticulous drawings for the main climbing guides. He once said to me: "There's no such thing as a bad day in the Lake District. The day is either wet or dry".

I asked Heaton Cooper what the average climber was wearing when he began climbing in the 1920s. He replied, with a smile: "I didn't know any average climbers. I only knew what I wore, which was ordinary tweeds and sweater—usually two sweaters".

He sometimes travelled by bus but more often it was on a bicycle or his two feet. He told me: "I very often had to run all the way down from Scafell Pike or Scawfell to the Old Dungeon Ghyll to catch the last bus home". When he bought a motor-bike, he was so ashamed of the noise the bike made that he soon gave it up.

John Bulman, a Langdale lad who grew up in the 1930s, saw a few "hikers" and cyclists. Motor cycle trials were held on the high passes. "We didn't think of the likely consequences and we all laughed at a drawing by Robert Spence showing Buttermere with a funicular on the fellside and double-decker buses going over Honister Pass".

After the 1939-45 war, said John, the number of visitors began to rise dramatically and the landscape suffered. There was "wild" camping, with tents pitched wherever people felt inclined. One party, who set up camp on the lawn of a house in Great Langdale, told the enraged householders—"you can't stop us; we're in a National Park".

In the 1960s there was an influx of working-class climbers: brave, competent men in the main, but in such numbers that they buzzed like flies round every suitable crag. "They had a lot of tackle," said John. "When I saw them coming down from the fell with their pitons, their nuts and bolts and spanners clanking, I was reminded of shire horses at an agricultural show. Climbing was an absolute craze at that time".

I had an affinity with Messrs Hardman and Wainwright because of my milltown background. Like them, I was able to spend an appreciable amount of my working life in Lakeland. For almost 40 years I had the joy of editing *Cumbria* magazine.

AW preferred to walk alone, in the spirit of Matthew Arnold when

17

he wrote of "the cheerful silence of the fells". Joe Hardman was happiest in some dalehead setting. He was not the fell-top type and rarely went more than 50 yards from a road.

Wainwright, a quirky, crochety, lovable man, has been with me in spirit while tackling the 214 Lakeland fells he featured in his seven guides and which now, of course, are known as "Wainwrights".

He was born at Blackburn in 1907. Despite the mean, Lowry-like setting and the abject poverty at home, he was an ambitious lad who was determined not to become mill-fodder. At the age of 13 he secured employment in local government, at 15s a week (which, as I once mentioned to him, was 2s.6d more than I got when I began work as a journalist at Skipton in the mid-1940s!).

The one aspect of Blackburn life that remained vivid in his memory was a football team, Blackburn Rovers. Each week, its exploits attracted the masses and relieved the sooty drabness. AW was present when Blackburn won th'cup in 1928.

He had his first memorable, lingering view of heaven, as represented by the Lake District, when he was 23 years of age. By that time he'd enough brass to go for a week's holiday in a far northern town called Windermere. Manfully, he staggered up Orrest Head, from which he had a grand prospect of Windermere.

He looked out across fields, lake, woodland and high hills and, as they say in Lancashire, he was "fair capped" or, in Biblical language, "sore amazed". Wainwright exulted and later wrote: "I never imagined there could be anything like that".

Now he was determined to have a heavenly life. In 1941, having been declared unfit for military service, Wainwright slipped into a minor job in the borough treasurer's department at Kendal, the old grey town by the Kent he came to love. When, six years later, he was appointed borough treasurer, his ambitions in local government had been met.

He was "Mr Wainwright" to the younger members of the staff. He never had much to say. He kept immaculate accounts, his ledgers being works of art because of the style and neatness of his script.

The workings of local government being very predictable, Wainwright invariably wrote up the minutes of a minor committee before it met. He was a great doodler and day-dreamer as the councillors

18

wittered on.

The councillors themselves saw a tall, grey, tweedy man. His staff noted that in all matters he was punctilious. He arrived at the office promptly at 9 a.m., went home for lunch for precisely one hour and, when the day's work was over, departed into obscurity unless there was an evening meeting to attend.

For a time, no one suspected the depths of his love for Lakeland. They did know that one of his desk drawers held pens, Indian ink and good quality paper because he was in the habit of giving drawings to his staff and friends on special occasions, such as weddings.

The drawings had such fine lines it was like looking at the best of Victorian engraving. He signed them A. Wainwright (A. being for Alfred). To inquirers he usually said "it isn't for Aloysius, if that's what you're thinking."

At Kendal, he was like Poo-bah, involved in dozens of worthy causes such as giving support to the old Kendal museum, where he spent hours writing labels for the specimens in the distinctive Wainwright script. Further hours were spent copying as line drawings some of the old photographs of the town. The photos might fade with time but, hopefully, the drawings would endure, especially as a selection was published.

In Lakeland proper, he was a man with a glorious anonymity. If anyone approached him, he slipped out of sight. If someone mentioned his name, he would shake his head and point out some fast-receding figure as the celebrated A. Wainwright.

He had a dry sense of humour. An inquirer into the effect his ceaseless penmanship was having on domestic affairs was told that it had proved too much for his wife, who one day went for a walk with the dog. Neither of them returned.

He admitted to being selfish where his pictorial guides were concerned. He was besotted with Lakeland and the work of recording all aspects of its mountain topography. He walked everywhere. His son, Peter, recalls, with a wince, when they set off from the house at Kendal and walked as far as Ill Bell. He would walk the full length of Longsleddale to reach the Nan Bield Pass.

When for some years he lived alone in the house on Kendal Green, it was almost too much of an effort to feed himself adequately. He had a standing order at the grocer's, augmenting this food with liberal helpings of shop-bought fish and chips, which were far and away his favourite food. Heaven must surely have a corner for a "chip shop".

Eventually, he was taken in hand—quietly, helpfully—by Betty McNally, whom became the second Mrs Wainwright. Betty was one person who did not stand in awe of him. And he was happy to leave organisational matters to her. She was his wife, housekeeper, chauffeur, proof reader, secretary and much else. AW could not imagine life without her.

Sharing a love of animals, they continued to provide a roof for cats, including a favourite animal which was tolerated on his desk or arching her back to rub herself against his arm as he drew or wrote. The margins of some of the drawings held paw-prints.

And together they worked for an animal charity, dealing with homeless and ill-treated dogs and cats. It was into the account of this charity that royalties from AW's books were paid.

This tall, bulky, pipe-smoking man with the shock of silver-grey hair and mutton chop whiskers, became a legend in his lifetime. The more he discouraged publicity, the keener was the Media to meet him.

He nonetheless "sat" for a sculptor who fixed his image, complete with pipe, in bronze. AW was a loner, lost in his own thoughts, not suffering fools gladly, speaking—Quaker style—only when the spirit moved him. He might, if he felt inclined, utter a few sentences now and again.

His fell-going days, during which he compiled the pictorial guides, were "the best years of my life". He tended to hide if he saw a crocodile of walkers approaching, not liking the idea of walking en masse and the tedious repetition of "hello" as the party went slowly by.

He turned down several requests to appear before the camera by remarking: "If I did, it would spoil everything..."

In his fell-going, he was like the Lakeland fell farmer—he travelled light, wearing above his everyday togs an old raincoat. He had no need of a large rucksack, carrying only his tobacco pipe, a camera, map or maps—and a bar of chocolate for sustenance. He did not normally carry a compass and, luckily, was never seriously in trouble when fell-wandering.

In 1986, AW ended his long years of obscurity by agreeing to appear in a television series. Simultaneously, he agreed to be interviewed by journalists, who had previously used his autobiographical book *Fell Wanderer* as a quarry for information about his life and outlook.

The man who achieved national fame as a pedestrian, artist, writer and television personality still found time to acknowledge many a written inquiry to his home with one of his distinctive notes, written in green ink. If the telephone rang when he was alone in the house— he ignored the summons.

As related, the vast sum of money generated by his literary activity was, in the main, directed towards charitable work, notably Animal Rescue Cumbria. As he put it: "One does not wish to be paid for writing a love-letter".

His later days were marked by impaired eyesight. It was a perennially misty Lakeland that confronted him. His last upland walk was on a wet day when it never stopped raining. "The mountains wept for me," he was heard to remark.

At home, sitting quietly, with smoke curling from his tobacco pipe, he went through the neat files of his mind and brought out delectable images of past excursions.

His poor eyes had been under severe strain for years. Some of his early line drawings were exquisitely fine. His seven-volume pictorial guide, on which he worked from 1952 until 1966, contains over 3,500 meticulously-drawn pictures of Lakeland mountain topography.

His *ad hoc* approach to the guides worked only because he was his own author, illustrator and book designer. His method "suited my particular circumstances and my own idea of the sort of book I would have liked for myself. . .I suppose you could say that was very self-indulgent, couldn't you?"

When he announced his retirement, and the *Westmorland Gazette,* his publishers for 30 years, wished to mark the occasion, Andrew Nichol, the book publishing manager, felt that AW himself should be left to decide what he should receive. It was a simple and inexpensive request—four Cornetto ice creams. Betty handed one to him at the time of delivery. She was about to give one to Andrew Nichol, when Wainwright said, a little gruffly: "Put the others in the fridge. They're my present and I'm going to enjoy them."

The Media now had ready access to the master fell-walker. When it was suggested to him that his highly popular guides had led to considerable erosion along the best-known Lakeland paths, he commented that it would have happened anyway as a consequence of the population having more money and leisure.

Like J B Priestley, he enjoyed his reputation for grumpiness and people re-told with a chuckle his semi-humorous comment that he preferred animals to people. He could be off-hand, even rude.

Sheila Richardson, writing in *Cumbria Life,* put the comment in its context. "Why animals?" she had asked. His reply was immediate: "They are so much nicer than people. They are loyal and honest, they don't pretend. They don't carry chips on their shoulders. They suffer in silence..."

AW died at Kendal a month later, on January 20, 1991, aged 84. The *Westmorland Gazette* headed its (lengthy) obituary with the words: "At peace with his fells". Richard North commented that the beauty of his books lay in their unique style and "in Wainwright's unquenchable love for his subject".

Paul Wilson, in *Outlook,* a newspaper supplement published in Wainwright's native East Lancashire, reminded us that Wainwright had not been content to stop once he had finished his series of pictorial guide books in 1966. He went on to provide guides to the Pennine Way, the Craven limestone country and Howgill Fells. He worked on large format sketchbooks of Lakeland, Bowland, some north-west rivers and Scottish mountains.

Harry Griffin, in *The Guardian,* began his tribute by describing AW as The Evangelist of Lakeland, "whose hand-written guides to pilgrims on the fells have sold more than a million copies..."

The Daily Telegraph obituary appeared under the heading "The man who walked to work" and a tribute in *The Yorkshire Post* echoed one of his choices in the radio programme Desert Island Discs—"The happy wanderer".

His ashes were scattered (at his express wish) by Innominate Tarn on Haystacks. There was a proposal to re-name the Tarn after him, but (happily) this was resisted.

Of all people, Wainwright would not like the idea of altering the map.

A Few Brief Encounters

He certainly opened up possibilities for many people, particularly the middle-aged and elderly who had thought that the high tops were for youngsters.

Eileen Jones, The Yorkshire Post, 1991

Pen Pictures from the Media

He produced meticulously hand-drawn maps and emotive prose purely for his own enjoyment...He called them love letters and they became best sellers though he never lifted a finger to promote them.

The Daily Mail

His wife, Betty, called him "Red" in memory of that once ginger hair that turned to a wispy white to match his downy whiskers.

The Independent

This old-fashioned mountaineer...went quietly about his job in much the same way as the great M J B Baddeley of the old red-backed Through Guides might have done...

The Guardian

He did not like change or technological progress. He even regarded the compass as an unfathomable gadget and refused to take one with him on the fells.

The Westmorland Gazette

I FIRST met him when he was Borough Treasurer with an office in an upper room at Kendal's Town Hall, with no better prospect from the windows than a row of business premises across a narrow street heady with traffic.

An interview had been arranged via Harry Firth, of *The Westmorland Gazette*. As related, Harry was in charge of the printing department, which had the contract for our two monthly magazines "The Dalesman" and "Cumbria" and was now about to print some unique little guides.

Several times a month I headed for Stricklandgate to visit that realm of hot metal and cold tea, where the head printer tut-tutted over bad grammar and typographical errors, such as "awful" for "lawful" and "rape recorder" for "tape recorder". Mr Mulligan's vigilance spared me many blushes on publication day.

When Harry Firth, visiting Clapham, opened a package and revealed the original art work of the first of the Wainwright walking guides which would be printed just as they were, without the addition of a single line of type, we marvelled. Each page was a compilation of drawing, map and incredibly small but legible hand-writing.

Wainwright's personal financial resources were nowhere near as large as the £900 or so the printer would charge to print and bind the book. He had asked a friend, Henry Marshall, the borough librarian, to allow his name to appear as the publisher, and it was Henry who told him to go ahead; he would foot the bill and Wainwright could pay him off from receipts.

Sensing that the publication would create a stir, I climbed the steps to his office with mounting excitement—and came away with no usable copy. Instead, AW quizzed me about the number of words and the type of illustration of the proposed feature.

After twenty minutes, it was clear that he wanted to retain his privacy. He did show me the contents of the top right drawer of his desk, which held some drawings.

So I went across Stricklandgate for a chat with Henry Marshall. Although it was the *Westmorland Gazette* machines that turned out the Wainwright books, initially the name Bateman and Hewitson (a firm absorbed by the group) appeared on the imprint.

With Harry Firth as an intermediary, I maintained a link with AW through the long years, during which we reproduced in our magazines (entirely free of reproduction fee) dozens of pages from the guides. AW got publicity and we got a worth-while feature.

Now and again I was tempted to use a photograph of Wainwright—a snapshot of his back and shock of white hair, with the bowl of his pipe showing at one side of his head. It was AW's ultra-private period and I left the photograph in the files.

Meanwhile, with the circulation of *Cumbria* keeping to a steady 15,000 I would go to the printing works, pass between white cliffs of paper earmarked for the Wainwright books and see machines chattering remorselessly to themselves as they put the imprint of alloy blocks on paper.

These in turn were replaced by lithography. The machines clattered on. I had a fanciful idea that the operatives had forgotten how to stop them.

AW retired from Kendal Corporation in 1967. He cleared out the drawers of his desk, walked out of the office and never returned. It was not a wholly happy time. His first marriage had been dissolved. Three years later, married to Betty, his personal happiness was restored.

I welcomed each new book and wrote a note about it for *Cumbria*. The review copies were all first-editions, which is why I do not expose them to the Lakeland weather on my outings.

Sometimes, having written a special piece about him, I submitted a draft by post. AW promptly returned it, having corrected any errors of grammar or spelling. He could not abide those who played fast and loose with English. One note (written with a metal pen in green ink) read: "Publish if you must".

When Harry Firth retired from the Gazette, a special meal was held at the Wild Boar Hotel and AW, who usually avoided such social occasions, recognised by his presence what Harry had done for him.

Andrew Nichol was now in charge of printing. He also ferried AW here and there when his presence was needed for special promotions. Andrew tried to incorporate in a trip across Cumbria a visit to a good fish and chip shop, such as the one at Ulverston, or even a Little Chef.

(When undertaking the coast-to-coast walk on "foot", for a BBC film, AW was shown partaking of haddock and chips in the shop at Kirkby Stephen which, by chance, stands almost exactly half way between the Irish and North Seas).

Television exposure did not cure him of his shyness but gave him a vastly greater audience. He was lucky for his BBC series to have the company of a few people who appreciated his temperament. He would not tolerate brashness nor hype.

The Lakeland landscape, despite many wet and windy days, was photogenic. AW did not care much for the use of incidental music, and would have preferred natural sounds.

For his Desert Island Discs programme, in which he was interviewed by Sue Lawley, he chose among other items The Happy Wanderer and a cowboy's lament for his dying horse. He wanted to take to his island a photograph of the cup-winning Blackburn Rovers team of 1928. He claimed that if he could not have a fish and chip shop, he would not survive a month.

On the day he recorded Desert Island Discs in Manchester—a special concession to him, for every other programme had originated in London—Andrew Nichol, when driving him back home could not resist a detour to take in Guiseley and Harry Ramsden's, the world's largest fish and chip shop. AW had his haddock and chips under crystal candelabra.

When he was 80 years old, his appearance belied his age. He and Betty visited the *Cumbria* office at Clapham; he had what we call in the North "a good colour" and beneath a veritable shock of white hair he had continued to indulge his love for pipe-smoking.

Yet he wheezed a little and was unsteady on the legs that had carried him so far across the fells. He confessed that his eyesight had deteriorated to the extent that he could no longer read newspapers. He was typing his books and letters as much by instinct as by sight.

The veteran fellsman had further books in mind and the continued interest of Totty, his favourite among the eight erstwhile stray cats that shared the facilities at his Kendal home.

After our conversation, we went to the Gamecock at Austwick for a simple bar-snack—cheese sandwiches, if I remember rightly—and then Betty drove us back to Clapham, with AW sitting in the back, his ample form spread across the car seat, his pipe producing as much smoke as a mill chimney and his smile indicating his pleasure at (being a back-seat rider) not having to wear a seat-belt.

I waved them farewell. They vanished Kendalwards in a fug of exhaust fumes and pipe smoke.

My last meeting with AW was at his home on Kendal Green—a home he had himself designed, striving to make it look older than it was. He was in the company of Derry Brabbs who was illustrating books he had written for publication by Michael Joseph.

I handed over a copy of my book *It's a Long Way to Muckle Flugga*, for which he had written the foreword, also a copy of *St Kilda: A Voyage to the Edge of the World*. Scotland's western seaboard fascinated AW. Betty would include the book in the list of works to be read to him now that his eyesight was impaired.

He introduced me to Derry mischievously as "the man who writes a book every ten minutes". I let my eyes range on the bookshelf containing evidence of his own prolific output.

Derry's introduction to the Lake District was "courtesy of AW". Knowing him as an outstanding landscape photographer, I had presumed he had been at work since the box brownie days of childhood. "Really and truly," said Derry, "until I got teamed up with AW I had not done any serious walking. So it is entirely due to him that I have been punished this way . . ."

He illustrated 18 of AW's favourite walks in the book *Fellwalking with Wainwright*. The collaboration continued. AW was in the habit of preparing his own page layouts, typing out the manuscripts and leaving spaces for photographs. "It made life very easy". The difficult bit was securing photographs of sufficiently high quality in a region where the mountains do not always lie in sunshine.

Derry, who was living at the village of Nidd, near Harrogate, had to travel about 75 miles to the heart of Lakeland. When I met him, he had spent two days camping in Langdale, waiting for a chance to go up Bowfell and carry on with some work on another Wainwright book. The weather was such that he got three passable photographs—for two day's work.

He never felt happy when on a steep scree and mentioned a winter day on Bowfell Buttress. He explored the Climbers' Traverse to the point where there is a huge scree run. It was covered with snow, which began to move as he walked across it. "I was rigid for about 10 minutes. Then I told myself that I would not achieve anything just standing there, so I went forward, clear of danger".

Wainwright achieved a special kind of fame in his own lifetime. He attended four sittings at the studio of Clive Barnard, the sculptor, with the result that a bronze was issued. This was not a bust but the whole man, sitting down, right hand on the ground, left hand attending to the pipe that AW habitually held.

One of the limited edition is in Kendal Museum. I remember seeing a copy displayed at Brantwood by Coniston Water. The effigy was so placed that AW was looking through a window straight across Coniston Water to the fells.

One Old Man surveyed another Old Man. The fell of that name had patches of snow in the cracks between its ancient limbs. Swirl How and Wetherlam completed a majestic trio.

All The Wainwrights

(from the pages of *Cumbria*)

Last year (1986) we heard of the remarkable
achievement of the Keswick dentist, Ian
Wallace, his wife and young family, who had
accomplished this feat within two years.

Then came the news that the great fell runner,
Joss Naylor, had actually done the whole of
the 214 tops in the incredible time of one
week, thus setting a record that can surely
never be broken.

I wonder if I might lay claim to a different kind
of record, namely, taking the longest time to
do all the Wainwrights. I began by climbing
Helvellyn in August, 1929, and completed the
course by climbing Slight Side in August of this
year, a span of 58 years.

Norman B Fishburn

It took me eight years to achieve this goal,
though in the early days I didn't go walking
with any particular end in view...Prize for
the least interesting Wainwright goes to
Mungrisedale Common, a shapeless heap of
moorland jutting out north of Blencathra. It
has one redeeming feature in that it can be
climbed via Sharpe Edge.

J S Barton (1976)

Wainwright and
the Animals

WE HEARD the radio transmission of *Desert Island Discs,* featuring AW, while sitting in a car at Long Marton, in the Eden Valley. The day's activity had been arranged with this broadcast in mind. We would have our major butty-stop within easy range of the car radio.

It was a depressingly wet and misty day. The humidity in the car was akin to that of a tropical rain forest. The windows suffered so much condensation they were like frosted glass. Here we were, in the "golden vale" between the Lakeland hills and the Pennines but with our visibility reduced to a few hundred yards.

We smiled as we heard the familiar voice telling his listeners he did not think there was any art about walking. Its a natural thing, he said, while cautioning people to watch where they were putting their feet when the temptation is to look at the view while walking along. We heard about the Wainwright Animal Trust, established with money he earned from his books.

We thought AW's choice of music was strange, to say the least. The only piece relating to animals, apart from an oblique reference to an elephant's eye in "Oh what a beautiful mornin'", was a cowboy's lament on the death of his faithful horse. We groaned.

AW and Betty came to see me at the offices of "Cumbria" early in 1988 and instead of talking about the fells I broached the subject of his animal charities.

Betty announced that she was going for a walk around Clapham village. Would he be all right for a while? AW said slowly, with mock gravity: "I think we'll have enough to talk about for twenty minutes or so. . ."

I knew he liked cats, especially Totty, his favourite among the eight erstwhile stray cats that shared the facilities at his home on Kendal Green, visiting his workroom and even sleeping on his bed.

AW was "a little frightened of dogs". He acknowledged the worthiness of the fell farmer's collie dog and its skill at rounding up sheep on hundreds of rough upland acres.

AW would have been the first to admit that he had no profound knowledge of natural history. He attempted to draw a golden eagle, to illustrate a page dealing with the Straits of Riggindale, but to me that eagle looked more like a barnyard fowl. He would have had some good close views of the common wren, a diminutive bird with turned up tail, which is at the other end of the size range.

I wondered if the buzzard he saw hovering motionless in the sky was not a kestrel, otherwise known as "wind-hover", though he had seen plenty of buzzards and they are clever at using the uplift of a wind against the crags. Ravens do engage in "tumbling flight".

In his slender booklet, *Old Roads of Eastern Lakeland*, he'd drawn quite convincing fell ponies, and the cover illustration showed a whole train of pack animals with attendant drovers. This booklet, published in 1985, was an astonishing achievement by someone whose eyesight was deteriorating.

AW felt compassion for the sheep, which he encountered at every outing. He saw them panting in summer heat and skulking behind the walls in driving rain or snow. Sheep, he considered, were too much at the whim of weather and economic conditions.

We chatted about red deer and foxes. He had seen both, of course, on many occasions, with the deer adorning the hills around Martindale and the "straight-necked" hill foxes giving sport to the six Lakeland packs of hounds.

AW did not care for hunting, but he was often aware of it during his winter walking as huntsman, whipper-in and umpteen couple of hounds swept the fellsides in a traditional ritual concerning pursuit and death.

AW returned to the plight of the ubiquitous hill sheep. Wainwright dedicated one of his pictorial guides to sheep!

He had presided for years over Animal Rescue Cumbria, a charity which promotes kindness and suppresses cruelty to animals, also seeking to open rescue centres for stray and unwanted animals and to look after them until new homes could be found.

An animal centre had been established at Kapellan, a Belgian word for "a bright place", this property being some four miles from Kendal. At the three branches of Animal Rescue Cumbria, over 12,000 animals have been found new homes.

Now he told me that the Charity Commissioners had recently approved the formation of the Wainwright Animal Trust, which was to receive the royalties earned by the seven pictorial guides published by the *Westmorland Gazette.* It would make grants half-yearly to animal welfare organisations in need of financial help.

Wainwright was in some respects like his fellow Lancashireman, the artist Lowry. Both could be irrascible and both cherished privacy, as evidenced by their work. Do any of the figures on a Lowry townscape overlap? And have you ever seen more than one person at a time on a Wainwright drawing?

Whereas Lowry might draw the odd "matchstick dog" to go with his "matchstick men", Wainwright often portrayed sheep. In his book *Fellwanderer,* which told the story behind the guides, he wrote about the sheep which shared the hills with him.

In particular, he commended their trod-making accomplishments, though a sheep track, while adequate for a sheep, was a wee bit narrow for the average walker who might otherwise have benefitted from it in rough terrain. Given the time, Wainwright hoped to plot sheep-tracks using field observations and a large-scale map of, say, Harter Fell, where he had noticed that sheep tracks were profuse.

He was tormented by thoughts of the cruelty man had meted out on birds and beasts, from the deliberate spread of myxomatosis to reduce the population of wild rabbits to the disposal of unwanted dogs by tossing them out of cars on motorways.

Hence his support of charitable work for animal welfare. He had the sufferings of animals on his mind to the end and there is a poignant passage on the subject in *Ex-Fellwanderer,* which was published to commemorate his 80th birthday.

A Ritual for Walking
Disciples of Wainwright

Scene: A narrow road between Ings and Troutbeck.
Time: Early morning in February, 1992.
Occasion: Travelling by car to where we will meet Stan.

BILL (talking into his microcassette recorder, of which he is very proud): We are now looking north-westwards and the hills are...

BOB (slowly and patiently): No, we're not looking north-westwards, Bill—we're looking across to the south-west of the Lakes.
(Bob draws the car to a halt and we admire a range of fells dusted lightly with snow. He begins a litany of Lakeland fell names).

BOB: You are looking at the Coniston group, with Coniston Old Man as the most southerly peak and then you're working round towards Brim Fell and the mass immediately in front of us is Wetherlam which, of course, you will remember...

BILL (to himself, as Bob drives on): Ah, yes—Wetherlam. Snow. Ice. Hailstones. Ice axe. And someone tripping up over his crampons.

BOB: ...and then you're swinging across towards the Crinkles and over to Bowfell and further round here you can see the Langdales...and Pavey Ark. Can you see the great black mass of Pavey Ark...

BILL: I remember it well, especially Jack's Rake. Now I know what a bat's thinking about when it hangs upside down.
(We turn into the Troutbeck Valley).

BOB: There's Ill Bell and its baby brother Froswick, which provides a mirror image...They lead on to High Street, where there are no shops.

(We meet Stan and Colin. Stan tries to sell us Great Gable—a painting, that is. We have what Bob calls a butty-stop, high on the fells. I ask Bob to define such a stop).

BOB: They come in two categories—minor butty-stops and major butty-stops. For a minor, you are allowed a cup of tea and one sandwich or a biscuit. A major butty-stop is a three-course meal. There's a star rating up to five, depending on the view and the weather. I don't think we've ever had a five-star butty-stop.

BILL (to Stan): You coined the word "touroid".

STAN: That is for one of the millions of people who visit the Lake District and walk no more than 60 yards, which is the average penetration of the district.

BILL: We've just passed what you call a "trog"?

STAN: That's a person who walks the fells with dozens of others as part of a long crocodile. He or she has over-sized boots and over-sized waterproof clothing. When you meet a trog on a narrow path you have to step off to let them pass.

BILL: What about the catch phrase (which is delivered staccato) "Does it get any better?"

STAN: It's said by one of the touroids who travel in thin shoes or sandals along the riverside path to Watendlath. When they meet a stream coming across the path they always ask the folk who are in proper gear: "Does it get any better a bit further on?"

BILL (into recorder): We are looking down on a buzzard...The lichened seat has been here since 1905...That isn't a cow taking its foot out of a swamp—it's Bob eating an apple.

(And so on. Hopefully, we are giving Alfred Wainwright a few chuckles as he sits on his celestial mountain top).

When Eyes Are Dimmed

IN APRIL, 1988, Dorothy Hemsworth sent a copy of a poem (author unknown) to Wainwright having heard of the decline in his eyesight:

> When the days come that I must live alone
> In my thoughts, and when my eyes are dimmed
> And cannot see the shadows on the hills
> Cast by the clouds, and when I cannot hear
> The far-off sounds of hurrying streams and sheep —
> Then I will turn my mind to those great days
> I spent upon the fells, and I will count them over, one by one
>
> I will remember rain and bitter winds,
> The feel of clothes drenched by stinging showers;
> Tea at a wayside inn with some good friends,
> Hot baths and fires, warmth for tired limbs,
> And all the loveliness of home and rest.
>
> And while I think of all those joyous days,
> Of all the heights I've gained, hours I've lived,
> I will not envy those who take their turn
> In tramping manfully in storm or fine
> The hills I know, for they are part of me —
> A heritage of beauty nought can spoil.

AW replied: "It is always a pleasure to hear from others who share my love of the Lakeland fells and northern hills, as you so obviously do...The lovely poem expresses my own feelings and sentiments so well. I will treasure this".

Some Favourite Mountains

(in no special order)

Ticking Them Off

Bob provided me with an annual report concerning my progress in bagging the "Wainwright" peaks.

Bob also mentioned some memorable moments, in particular a January day when northern byroads were plated with ice and "I drove in conditions which varied from bad to ludicrous".

"May 5 found Stan, plus John (his son-in-law), you and I, on Moor Divock, looking for shops on the High Street".

WRM

Fairfield and Company:

A "Red Mist" Job

A TELEPHONE call from Bob in January informed me that his son Michael was about to complete his round of the Wainwrights. He had only two or three to capture. Would I like to join the party for the last glorious stretch? It would, said Bob, be little more than a stroll.

I knew enough about the Wainwrights—and about Bob—to doubt his assessment of the expedition as a "stroll". Wainwrighting is usually hard work.

Alan Heaton, celebrating the 25th anniversary of his entry into the Bob Graham 24 Hour Club, had wiped them all off by travelling from dawn to dusk. He completed the entire round in 9 days, 14 hours, 42 minutes. In 1986, the legendary Joss Naylor, aged 50, ran the Wainwright Round of 391 miles, climbing a total of 121,000 feet, in 7 days, 1 hour, 25 minutes.

Bob did not intend to ask for this sort of performance from me—yet. It was to be a two-car job, he said. And so it was, one car being left beside Dunmail Raise and the second being brought to a halt in the car park just across the road from the Traveller's Rest on Kirkstone Pass, in an area where Lakeland is at its greyest, sharpest and knobbliest—a primeval scene of knolls and tumbling becks.

Harriet Martineau, in a shilling guide published last century, described what could be seen from Kirkstone and added: "Near at hand, all is very wild...and the Kirkstone mountain has probably mists driving about its head."

As I donned my boots, there was time to ponder on the Traveller's Rest, a low white building on what appears to be a ledge cut out of the rock. When I first knew it, the Atkinsons lived here. They had bought it in 1914 and, Sherpa-like, had tuned their breathing to the rarefied conditions.

They lived between walls which are three feet thick and under a heavy slate roof, but were still conscious of the wind. At Kirkstone, Pat Leighton the postman was blown over a wall. He was not upset by the experience. This Postman Pat was still delivering mail on his 81st birthday.

I wondered if the ghost of Old Jerry, the coach-driver, still haunts Kirkstone. In his day there was a close season for storming the passes with a coach and six. The season ended in September, whereupon Jerry wintered at Salford, in darkest Lancashire.

When the weather was grim, he would contrast it with that on Kirkstone Pass, saying to his friends: "Aye, aye, it's grey dowly on Kirkstone Pass noo; there's snow in the road and the wind's roaring— roaring like a lost bairn on Red Screes". Or words to that effect.

Standing in the car park opposite the Traveller's Rest, I had to tilt my neck in order to take in the full grandeur of a fell which rises to 2,547 ft and is much more than the corrie with the scree-slope after which it is named.

As I climbed, I stopped ever more frequently to admire the view and the tiny white box far below which was in reality the inn. Half an hour later, suffering from middle age, under-exercise and excessive smoking, with a preference for Woodbines, I knew why my Scottish friend George refers to an abrupt frontal attack on a mountain as "sudden death". And, when a rush of capillaries cloud the vision, why Stan refers to such an experience as "a red mist job".

It was like climbing a big red wall except that my booted feet did not seem to want to stay where I put them. Wainwright had explained this instability by mentioning two combes which had carved deeply into the mountain. They were now sprinkling it with red particles. Rocks and soil had the dull reddish tint of old firebricks.

I cleared the top with some relief, thankful that Bob had not in-sisted on going up Middle Dodd using a route which Wainwright said should be followed only by those with a surplus of energy. "They will get rid of it on this treadmill".

I had no sooner put my stone on the cairn, bagging my first Wain-wright, than I had to develop a jog-trot to catch up the others, who were collecting a few slightly lower Wainwrights between here and Hartsop.

The "stroll" continued with the higher parts of the Fairfield Horseshoe, which goes round the head of Rydal Beck. At Fairfield himself—Wordsworth's "mighty" Fairfield—a grassy pate extended to an elevation of 2,863 ft.

I was not in the mood for talk, walking as though in a trance, with my flabby leg muscles tightening up like violin strings on the upward stretches and being allowed to relax a little on the down gradients.

The weather was generally dull, though bright over Morecambe Bay to the west. The sky held cloud of a dozen shades of grey. Occasionally, beams of sunshine appeared, like spotlights at a theatre.

Wordsworth, who was fond of mentioning the transient nature of Lakeland weather, would have enjoyed this cocktail of drizzle or sleet being delivered by clouds of various shades of grey on to an icy ground.

Bob announced that Seat Sandal, his son's last Wainwright, was "not so far away". It involved a dramatic descent from Fairfield followed by a tiring "up and over" on Seat Sandal, with ravens for company.

We glimpsed Thirlmere and toasted the achievement of young Michael before descending warily in semi-darkness to where we had left a car. It was reached in the last glimmer of daylight. I am sure that if it had been parked 100 yards further on, we would not have found it.

The air was still. If it had not been January, we might have been tempted to stay on the fell all night and greet the dawn from a high vantage point. Wainwright found that the experience of being on a Lakeland fell at night was profound: it attuned him to the mountains until he felt to be a part of the living rock.

Helm Crag:
Midget of a Mountain

HAVING stood on the topmost rock of Helm Crag, above Grasmere, I returned safely—swaggeringly, indeed—to my rucksack for a celebratory drink of thermos tea. As I drank, a passing raven flicked over on its back, giving me a "victory roll".

It was on the eve of my 64th birthday that I accomplished a fell-going feat which had eluded Mr Wainwright. He made several unsuccessful attempts to surmount the highspot. Wainwright's efforts were defeated "by a lack of resolution", to use his own words.

It eluded him despite his description of the shapely Helm Crag as "a midget of a mountain".

When I thought that the worst parts of Helm Crag were over—and it is a fairly stiff fell to climb—Bob pointed to a pinnacle at one end of the almost level ridge and remarked: "Just nip up there".

I do not normally use the word "nip" on the Lakeland fells. The word is not entirely suited to humbling the bungalow-sized boulders on the skyline of Helm Crag. Chris Bonington would have run up the rocks, but for me it was a major feat of acrobatics.

The first problem was how to make peace with the young couple who were sitting on the rocks at the start of the climb. They were about to feed their baby which had been travelling, Indian papoose style, on the lady's back. She had gone through the preparations for feeding, and had poured milk from a thermos flask into a feeding bottle. This young mother tested the temperature by squirting some on to the back of her hand as I approached amid a clatter of displaced stones.

The adults were quite nice about my intrusion, though the baby, which had gone through lip spasms as it quested for something to suck, objected with a loud cry. When both the child and the parents had moved a few yards and were pacified, I clambered upwards,

44

using hand holes which had become smooth with over-use, embracing fat boulders and lodging feet into cracks of unhandy sizes.

Eventually, I had the courage to stand, not in triumph—with the Vale of Grasmere appearing to be at my feet—but so that Bob could see me. He waved and ticked off yet another name from the list of "Wainwrights".

We had approached Helm Crag deviously, walking up Far Easedale and having a "butty stop" on Calf Crag—nothing special, mind you, and most certainly nothing to compete with the provisions consumed by 18th century visitors, Captain Joseph Budworth and friends just before they climbed the hill.

They consumed "stuffed roast pike, a boiled fowl, vealed cutlets and ham, beans and bacon, cabbage peas and potatoes, anchovy sauce, parsley and butter, bread and cheese, wheatbread and oat-cake, three cups of preserved gooseberries with a bowl of rich cream..."

Bob and I listened to the gruff voices of the ravens which were playing hide and seek in the mist. Wordsworth, in a piece about tarns, mentioned the gruff-voiced birds which are still quite common in Lakeland:

> The crags repeat the raven's croak
> In symphony austere:
> Thither the rainbow comes, the cloud,
> And mists that spread the flying shroud,
> And sunbeams, and the sounding blast.

Of course, I did not want to upset the birds by reciting this piece aloud. Bob and I drank from our thermos flasks and headed southwards, being overtaken by noisy chevrons of grey geese which were doubtless switching their grazings from Solway to the Kent Estuary, using the central route.

We saw at close quarters the strange assortment of big rocks on the ridge of Helm Crag. A Victorian walker, Mrs Linton, looking down from Fairfield saw "little Helm Crag, crested with its strange stone feathers".

Towards the end of the 18th century, at the start of what was to become known as the Romantic Age, a visitor to Helm Crag was Joseph Budworth, who—arriving before people had begun to put names to individual stones—compared the summit rocks to "a grand ruin, occasioned by an earthquake, or a number of stones jumbled together after the mystical manner of the Druids".

Victorian travellers, while being driven up Dunmail Raise in one of Mr Rigg's coaches, hauled by six horses, heard the driver tell fanciful tales of the curiously-shaped rocks on Helm Crag. Johnnie Greenbank was among the most characterful of those drivers. He could talk as well as drive. It was said of him that he could handle his team of four so well that it would not matter if it consisted of "three blinnd 'uns and a bolter".

The coach drivers named the rocks crowning Helm Crag and those names varied a good deal until they had been fixed in guide books. At one end of the ridge was a Lion Couchant which was also, from certain angles, "The Old Woman Playing an Organ". At the other end stood The Lion and the Lamb, a most popular feature because it could be seen from Grasmere and as the drive up Dunmail Raise continued the Lion "ate" the Lamb.

On Dunmail Raise, in the summer of 1904, motorised coaches raised the dust. The first of the Yellow Perils arrived on the Windermere-Keswick route and the experiment was noted in *The Westmorland Gazette*. The experiment proved so successful "as to encourage those who undertook the enterprise to place orders for numerous steam motor-cars to be employed during the coming season on this route and possibly in other directions in the Lake District".

Wainwright lived to see Dunmail Raise re-modelled, widened and thronged with infernal-combustion engines. He died without climbing over the Lion's mane. He must have felt frustrated, though he did not have the figure for rock-climbing and he acknowledged that this is one of the very few summits in Lakeland reached by climbing rocks.

On the page in his pictorial guide relating to the view from Helm Crag, Alfred Wainwright left a postage-stamp-sized space for an announcement that he had succeeded in surmounting the highest point. In the first edition, he wrote somewhat glumly: "Up to the time of going to press, however, such an announcement cannot be made."

Taming the Lion added lustre to my own achievements. I was proud of myself until Bob said: "Don't dawdle up there. You've umpteen more Wainwrights to do. . ."

Wetherlam:

An Ice-axe Job

BOB and I ticked off the Old Man in summer and one of its neighbours, Wetherlam, in winter. We had seen the saddleback ridge when afar off. The approach to this northern outlier of the Coniston group, which many claim to be superior to the Old Man—if lacking his height—was across ground that held the russet tones of old vegetation.

Wetherlam is composed of volcanic rock. A visitor might expect to find it still warm after its fiery baptism, but at the time of our visit the fell was plated with ice. The clouds brought hailstones, not rain.

Wainwright likened the 2,502 ft Wetherlam to a whale—a "giant whale surfacing above waves of lesser hills". It is also a somewhat battered whale, bearing the scars of quarrying and levels which were left by copper miners.

He drew some of the man-made entry points to the green heart of Wetherlam—the quarries, many like sores on the hillsides but some like Black Hole Quarry impressing by the sheer scale of working and, in this case, an enormous arch.

The first time I used an ice-axe for its intended purpose was on Wetherlam. There was no hint of arctic conditions as we parked near Tilberthwaite, in the tropical zone, and headed northwards with the tang of woodsmoke from a local farm to tickle our nostrils.

We strode on a path cut from the hillside above the romantic, secret world of Tilberthwaite Gill, which runs up towards Wetherlam. Last century, the hardiest of tourists could venture there because wooden bridges were placed to link up paths as scary as goat-tracks. None of the bridges remain. The walkers wisely keep to their high level route and in spring may hear the cool fluty whistle of a ring ouzel—our "northern nightingale".

The path we followed was through open country which that day was being over-run by the disciples of John Peel and their hounds (not dogs!). When the hunt had swept by, we meandered then climbed with the bare bones of the landscape sticking out in lichened splendour. During the unrelenting haul to the skyline, conditions slowly became more spartan.

Then came the moment when Bob fitted crampons to his boots and removed the protective piece of rubber from the spike of his ice-axe prior to using it. Flexing his wrist, he advanced with a clumping gait, as though he was a computer which had been programmed to tackle hills.

It seemed over-dramatic until, on reaching the frozen, hail-sprinkled lower slope, I did a three-point landing, the third point being my head. Now the ice-axe was in use. With fresh confidence, and a mental image of Everest against which to act out my fantasies, I started cutting my stairway to heaven.

Pausing for breath in the snowy and also misty conditions—it was like wandering about in an open refrigerator—I concentrated for a short time on action near at hand, such as the rate that hailstones were filling up the deep hole left by the shaft of Bob's ice-axe.

It was an anti-climax when we went over the rim and found the summit, to go through the stone-setting ritual of claiming another Wainwright. We classified the climb as "hairy".

The top of the fell had affinities with a skating rink. I made a resolution to return another day and look for yet another Lanty Slee's Cave. The indispensable Wainwright had marked it clearly on his map of the fell.

The Nab:
Retreat For the Red Deer

WAINWRIGHT was not over-sensitive about sticking to rights of way; in his day, ramblers were not yet moving about in hordes and most farmers and landowners were benign. Yet even Wainwright was aware of the very special—very private—status of The Nab, at the heart of the Martindale Deer Forest.

He mentioned the "keep out" notices, the barricaded gates and barbed wire which even the dullest of walkers would surely recognise as a deterrent. The Nab is a hallowed part of the only ground in England where red deer are stalked, as in Scotland. The deer deserve their refuge, even if they can no longer be guaranteed quietness in a period of low-flying jet aircraft. During the 1939-45 war, the Army used the area for manoeuvres.

AW did attain the grassy summit of the fell, of course. He acknowledged in the appropriate pictorial guide that he had trespassed and did not write for permission to climb the Nab through fear of being refused. He sneaked in and was undetected possibly, as he wrote, because of his marked resemblance to an old stag!

My first acquaintance with Martindale came many moons ago when the north-west branch of the British Deer Society held field meets up there, led by Peter Delap, who knew the deer as individuals, and with Mrs Delap providing a substantial afternoon tea in the kitchen of the White House, in Boroughgate, Appleby.

Martindale is a secluded little valley, reached by following a road from Pooley Bridge—a road which has not outgrown its old status of country lane—and then from Howtown climbing the zig-zags of the Hause.

One has a choice of two valleys and Martindale itself splits into two, with Bannerdale and Rampsgill, the Nab soaring in between. We deer-watchers climbed to The Bungalow (Lord Lonsdale's tin shooting lodge), and saw the large weather vane, a necessity in stalking country where the wind must fan the face, not tickle the back of the neck, if a stalker is to approach deer undetected.

The Nab soared to a slender cone. The deer were living up to their name when they had the redness of the summer coat. Add to deer-sightings, the sounds of wild birds—raven's croak and falcon's chatter—and Martindale became a magical place, especially if a golden eagle appeared to view. With a party of sharp-sighted deermen, it was unlikely to escape detection, even if it was little more than a dark speck seen against the underbelly of a passing cloud.

There's little point in climbing the Nab unless a "Wainwright" is to be ticked off. Most of the Bannerdale flank can be seen from the path represented on the map by a dotted green line extending from Dale Head to Boredale Hause.

Once, intent on "mopping up" some Wainwrights and at the same time watching the late summer sun rise over Ullswater, we parked the car just off the road to Sandwick and took the rising ground to Sleet Fell. (There was not even a glimmer of sunlight: just a steady seepage of grey light under the cloud mass).

Hart Crag seemed an appropriate setting for deer, but none was seen. Boredale Hause offered only sheep and a pony. Then we swung down into Martindale and, lo, red stags were moving with their distinctive haughty gait against the dramatic upswing of the Nab.

With permission, one may go up the Nab. When I first knew Martin-dale, I would call to see Joe Wells of Thrang Crag, who reared a stag calf in a croft near his home. Those who walked or drove up the dale saw the local version of the Monarch of the Glen. At night, the deer sneaked down off the hills into the best fields as they greened-up after their winter chilling.

We confirmed Wainwright's observation that the dome of the Nab was grassed over. "A few stones have been carried up and make an untidy cairn," he reported. There were also peaty areas where the big stags might wallow.

Up here, in a world composed of ice-smoothed peaks, ridges and corries, the old Lakeland asserted itself. Climbing from Hartsop in autumn, I had listened to the bellow of stags in the echo-chambers of the deep valleys. (The Scots call the bovine calls "roaring").

The Scottishness of the Martindale deer country once prompted Col-in to produce photo-copies of two letters Wainwright had written to a "Mr Green", a fan who had successfully assaulted the fearsome Aonach Eagach ridge above Glencoe. The original letters had slipped from a second-hand book which Colin had bought.

Writing "c/o The Westmorland Gazette" on August 4, 1974, AW offered congratulations and confessed that "I have had my sights on it for donkey's years but never ventured to attempt it. I have grown old looking at it from a safe distance, and now the effort is beyond me...There are still stirrings of life in me. In June I climbed two Munro's in the Glen Affric area. Easy ones. Nothing like Aonach Eagach".

AW had mentioned to "Mr Green" a forthcoming book of Scottish drawings which would include a study of the mountain. Rather more than a year later, Mr Green reminded AW of his promise to let him have a copy. He apologised for the delay; the task had been held up for more than a year "by a desire to do a sort of requiem for dear-departed Westmorland" (an enormous task!).

AW indicated that he was planning to go to Glencoe to finish off the fieldwork for that area. As hotel charges were "getting out of hand", he had booked a caravan and he would be in touch with Mr Green in a few months "if I survive the caravan".

In Glencoe, AW doubtless saw plenty of red deer and may possibly have been reminded of Martindale, where the 19th century cult of the deer forest, supported enthusiastically North of the Border by Victoria and Albert, was much in evidence.

It was the time when Highland estates had lodges as big as town houses. No effort was spared to make them imposing. I entered one semi-ruined Victorian lodge where the ceilings looked to be finely plastered but were composed of zinc.

Visitors to such lodges passed thickets of antlers made up as seats and hat-racks and eventually came under the beady gaze of deer heads set in neat rows on the lofty walls above the grand staircase.

During the stalking season, well-to-do folk followed professional stalkers by bog and ben. In their quest for "good heads" they were slowly eaten alive by insects under grey skies at what is often the stormiest time of the year.

After visiting the Nab, it was appropriate to go to Dalemain, where the big house (open to the public at prescribed times) was built around a pele tower. For over 300 years the Hasell family have presided over Dalemain.

In the old days, I enjoyed having a chat with Major Hasell and on one occasion his widow gave me a special tour of the house, including a glimpse of a door lock, complete with key, and four-poster bed, given to the family by Lady Anne Clifford, in whose service the

Hasells moved when entering into their present estate.

The Hasells acquired land in Martindale in about 1690 when Sir Edward bought Winter Crag, subsequently acquiring by marriage the Manor of Martindale, including the dalehead farm and 20,000 acres of unenclosed fell.

The indigenous deer represented protein on the hoof, with the appeal of fresh meat in the depth of winter. At the Boon Hunts, the tenants did service for the lord, driving the deer from the periphery of the forest into Bannerdale, where slaughter took place. (The same sort of thing happened in nearby Wet Sleddale, where the Lowthers had a large circular holding area for deer).

The family's lively pack of buckhounds hunted deer or fox with equal zest. In the 1820s, when Martindale was the only deer stalking forest in England, guests were accommodated in the hotel at Howtown, known at that period as the *Stag Inn*.

During what has been called the Edwardian Sunset, the Yellow Earl (of Lonsdale) took the lease of Martindale and—with no expense spared, here and on adjacent holdings—developed the deer forest idea to its ultimate, entertaining no less a celebrity than the Kaiser.

The first building to be erected by the Yellow Earl was the so-called Lowther House, which was miles from anywhere on the High Street range. There followed the "tin" bungalow at the head of Martindale, where the Nab forms a splendid backdrop. The lodge is of Bavarian design and was assembled here by an Austrian workman.

This structure, which still stands, appeared in 1910. It was designed for two gentlemen who wished to stalk; there were two master bedrooms, with separate bathrooms (cast iron baths!) and a verandah from which the fells could be contemplated. Staff quarters were included.

In due course, the Yellow Earl's trustees called a halt to much of his expenditure. He gave up the lease of the forest in 1933. By this time, the Hasells were having their sport disturbed by "numerous hikers" and by "stray hounds from a meet in Mardale".

As we left the dale, I chuckled at the recollection of driving a yellow car up Martindale. For yellow was associated in the minds of older dalesfolk with Lord Lonsdale.

One of the farmers remarked: "Nay—I thowt Owd Lordy was coming back agin".

Scafell:
A Long Slog

A PERCEPTIVE Victorian writer, Mrs. Linton, referred to "the tremendous steeps of Scawful". Wainwright, though aware of the majesty of the fell's huge western flank, singled out "the towering rampart of shadowed crags" in the north and east.

Bob, on an excursion to Wasdale Head, pointed to Scawfell and remarked: "One day, we'll get up early, give ourselves a treat and go in by the back door".

And so it was that we Wainwrighters stayed overnight at Stan's and celebrated our achievement in advance by having a candlelit meal in a hotel by Solway Firth. The next day was already "far spent" when we parked the car near the bottom of Hardknott Pass and strode by Brotherilkeld, the topmost farm in Eskdale.

The old folk in Eshd'l call the farm Butterilket. They are inclined to take short-cuts when pronouncing names. Repeat Brotherilkeld several times until you have mentally assimilated that awkwardly-placed letter "l". Like so many of the upland farms of Lakeland, the name is Norse, said to mean "summer farm of Ulfkell". The landlord is the National Trust.

On a misty day in a depressingly cloudy summer, we were among a few walkers who left behind the Eskdale of tarmac and motor traffic for an upper dale where tumbling water was busily putting the finishing touches to the landscape.

In the Middle Ages, the site of Brotherilkeld farmhouse was chosen by Cistercian flockmasters to accommodate shepherds. These Lakeland fells are sheep-sick. The Esk still flows cold and clear, between banks adorned by bracken and oak trees.

Having "done" Scafell Pike, the attic of England, by the main routes, we were intent on covering five miles through a roadless area

53

to Scafell, Lakeland's second highest fell. At first, the deep, rounded and relatively smooth valley was a reminder of the grinding power of the valley glacier of old.

If we thought of ice, it was only as a source of refreshment on a hot day when even the shorn Herdwick yows seemed uncomfortable. Red marks on nape and shoulder identified them as local sheep.

Noises from Yew Crag signified that there was a territorial dispute between buzzards and crows. Bell heather decked the ledges on a 30 ft deep gorge cut by the Esk. Wheatears chacked and whistled. A dragonfly with an especially large head and a black, white-banded body patrolled near Throstlegarth Bridge, spanning Lingcove Beck, which provides the Esk with an infusion of oxygenated water by way of a series of cascades.

Leaving the U-shaped glacial valley behind, we entered the country of deep gorges, climbing beside the Esk gorge which Dudley Hoys, the Eskdale writer, used to think of as a barbarous and beautiful prelude to Upper Eskdale. The misted fells reminded me of Victorian prints. Our 19th century ancestors liked a touch of melancholy on their out-door excursions.

At Great Moss, over 1,000 ft above sea level, insects began to draw our blood. Some outstanding specimens of bog-cotton in the wettest places resembled sticks of candy-floss. Scafell (pronounced Scawfell) was capped with mist, through which came the hoarse calling of the raven.

The damp ground was enlivened by the gold of bog asphodel. We crossed one tract of boggy ground on a path beside a ruined wall which is said to have been built in monastic times to retain deer. Perhaps.

So to Cam Spout, which was also named by the Norse settlers, ''cam'' being their term for ridge. The attendant scramble, partly on loose stones and partly on naked rock, was just a hard slog. When we stopped, it was to survey a misted summer landscape, with its austere but green hills and the silver gleam of water. No wonder the settlers whose ancestors had lived in Scandinavia felt at home in these parts.

On to Mickledore. With Cam Spout behind us, we had a respite before making yet another ascent, this time over boulder-strewn ground. The mist rolled away. Scafell's topmost rocks appeared to view, looking as awesome as the North Wall of the Eiger (though in fact it was the East Buttress we had in view).

Had we worked so hard to achieve so little? The seriousness of the situation was reflected in Bob's switch from tea to an orange, for extra energy.

We might have used the gully to Foxes Tarn but decided to prolong the agony and see Scafell at its most majestic, continuing to struggle up the boulder-littered slope to Mickledore, between Scafell and Scafell Pike. A sprinkling of visitors who had toiled up from Wasdale turned left for the higher peak.

Curiously, the Wasdale side of Mickledore was blotted out by mist and our side was clear. Bob and Stan told blood-curdling stories of Broad Stand, at the far end of the Mickledore traverse, where progress from a rock platform to moderately sloping ground is halted by some 30 ft of rock passable only to well-equipped climbers. We consulted Wainwright. He had drawn Broad Stand with a sign marked "Not for Walkers".

We begrudgingly gave away some of our hard-earned height, then gained it in stages, using Lord's Rake. a hundred yards of hard labour which, said Bob, is easier in deep snow. He paused for effect and added "...which I have seen in July. This section faces north and is sheltered from the sun".

At first glance, the gap between the main crag and subsidiary buttress, with its litter of boulders, seemed too steep for comfort.

We scrambled upwards to where the going was narrow and even steeper, with comparatively few good handholds and took the West Wall traverse, a steep scramble over loose rock, which leaves the rake just before the second col.

Finally, the crossing of a boulder-field brought us pantingly to the summit where Colin sighted—a spider. He speculated about the way it would descend from the summit. Would it spin a silken thread—and abseil?

We scanned the misted landscape and saw a gleam on Wastwater and Burnmoor Tarn. From Horn Crag (Slight Side), with the cloud drifting away and sunlight burning up the remaining mist, we felt we could see forever. In view was a grand assembly of high fells, with not a person in sight! The only hint of the modern world was in the occasional bright patch as a car descended Hardknott Pass.

The Lintons, visiting Scawfell from Wasdale in the 1860s, slept on the top, watched the sunrise in the morning and descended into Wasdale, "passing the terrible gap of Mickledore...then down by the beck and over a long stretch of wet grass, winding up and over another shoulder, and by loose screes and broken rocks, to get entangled in a labyrinth of walls and watercourses and sheep-tracks and delusive paths".

Our way down to Eskdale was a pleasant route, first on grass, then across a terrain of peat and heather.

We glimpsed Brotherilkeld, far below us. Our moment of deliverance came as we settled under roadside trees, with our rucksacks as pillows, and waited for a selfless and still energetic Colin to jog to the dalehead to collect the car.

The Tongue:

Soggy Hump in Troutbeck

WAINWRIGHT'S introductory drawing to his section on Troutbeck Tongue is the familiar view from the Windermere-Kirkstone road.

It is a good viewpoint, if you can stand the traffic—the motor coaches, cattle wagons and Land Rovers in which farmers and collies sit gravely side by side.

The Kirkstone road sometimes holds a flock of sheep. The shepherd, with his light alloy crook, sits on one of those mechanical scooters built by the Japanese to save his footwear. The engine clatters, the sheep baaa and hard cleaves beat a tattoo on the road. If I interpret the look on the collie's face a-right, it is enjoying every minute of its ride as pillion passenger.

That is what happens on one side of the wall. On the other side, all is peace and rural beauty. The land falls away steeply. A buzzard mews as it wheels over the thin woodland. In the middle distance, dwarfed by much higher ground, is the Tongue, a modest 1,191 ft hump, humbled by the grey-green humps of Yoke, Ill Bell and Froswick.

On Wainwright's drawing, the only dwelling is Troutbeck Park, set against a web of drystone walls, which form a futuristic pattern in the upper dale. We combined a mopping up of fells lying south of the Garburn Pass with a visit to The Tongue, which both of us had climbed in our younger days. The Garburn Road, to use a grand old name, connects Troutbeck and Kentmere, between which it attains 1,450 ft. We scanned the Troutbeck Valley. The Tongue was like a huge carbuncle sprawling across the upper dale.

The Garburn was exceptionally busy that day. We went clatteringly up the lane which begins not far from Troutbeck Church. A farmer with a brown-and-white collie told us that this dog was from a type bred in the district for at least 60 years.

The collie, an Artful Dodger, rounded up some sheep. It responded to short, unemotional whistled commands of the man. Not long before we had chatted with a fell farmer who also had a white stick. He explained that the dog could clearly see it when he held it up, responding to the stick as enthusiastically as it did to whistling.

"Aye," said the old man, "yon stick cost me nowt. I git it oot of a hedge and shaved it till I could see t'white pith. It's useful when I'm driving sheep on t'road. Folk think I'm half-blind!"

Troutbeck village, beheld from Applethwaite Quarry, was seen to retain its olde-worldiness, having been by-passed. The township was once divided into "hundreds", hence the local chant:

Three hundred brigs of Trout,
Three hundred bulls,
Three hundred constables,
And several hundred fools.

Back in the Valley, we walked steadily northwards, silenced by the sheer beauty of this little dale, with its green fields, fellsides that held the copper tone of dead bracken and grassy uplands. Here were field barns, gin-clear becks, gills, a scattering of trees, buzzards and sheep, lots of sheep, with two breeds represented: Swaledale (known to the Lakeland farmer as Sward'l) sheep and herdwicks (which were the favourites of a former owner of Troutbeck Park, a certain Mrs Heelis).

Perhaps you had wondered how long it would be before I mentioned Mrs Heelis, who before her marriage to Willie Heelis, a Lakeland solicitor, was known as Miss Beatrix Potter, creator of the small picture books in which animals dress-up and talk. Beatrix bought Troutbeck Park in 1923 and visited it regularly in a chauffeur-driven car.

There was Life before Beatrix, of course. Wainwright devoted four pages of the appropriate pictorial guide to Troutbeck Tongue but did not once mention her. And in the pre-Beatrix Potter period, these wave-like fells were "calm", according to the quotable Mrs Linton (1864). "The valley, now so bare of trees, was once so thickly wooded that the old inhabitants used to say a squirrel could have passed from the lake side [Windermere] to Threshthwaite Mouth [up by Thornthwaite Crag] without once touching the ground".

We discussed Beatrix Potter over a cup of tea, enjoyed where we could peer over the wall and across a field to the farmhouse in front of which her posh car was occasionally parked. She was an outdoor person who preferred to sit out on the Tongue rather than round the table in the kitchen of the farmhouse.

Neither of us had been impressed by the actual summit of the Tongue and Wainwright referred to a "grassy knoll" graced by a small heap of stones. It was the view from the Tongue that appealed to him. This dollop of rock and water-logged ground does provide good grazing, even in drought, for the sheep and a few wintering deer.

Most of my information about the Tongue came from two men who knew Mrs Heelis well—Tom Storey, who was her shepherd at Troutbeck Park before taking over at Hill Top, Sawrey, and Anthony Benson, who worked at the Park for a long period. Beatrix was recalled by Tom as "a little woman, and bonnie-looking".

Tom's sojourn at Troutbeck Park was brief but happy. "It was her pet farm, though she didn't often enter the house. . She'd take a sandwich with her and go for a walk on to the fell. She'd go to Tongue End and wait for me coming back with the sheep. I'd sit with her for a while and tell her all that had happened. It was not often she could be persuaded to come into the farm kitchen for a drink o' tea. She just had her sandwiches, which were lapped in a piece of paper. She ate 'em outside".

Anthony told me of the collie dog Bob, "a lile bow-legged thing, though he'd bin a good dog in his time." Though Bob was "a useless old thing", she insisted that Anthony should take it with him for a walk. One day, Bob went along a sheep trod and did not return. "We wasted many a day looking for it. Mrs Heelis came up every day to help. But Bob was not seen again".

Does Bob's ghost haunt the Tongue, this strange hump of a hill in the upper valley? As a vantage point it is limited to a grand view to the south—a view of the middle and lower reaches of the Troutbeck Valley and of Windermere, gleaming between its low Silurian hills.

All In The Mind

THE fells are a marvellous tonic. There is no doubt they can help people. I have never felt "down" or depressed when I have been up here.

On meeting a woman suffering from depression who had been inspired, by his books, to climb Scafell, 1990.

I HAVE found the pen, in my hands, no instrument for describing the captivating charms of Lakeland. It's an emotion and emotions are felt, not expressed.

At the launch of "Fellwalking with Wainwright", 1984.

Skiddaw:
Keswick's Mighty Mountain

MY LEG muscles, now as taut as violin strings, told me I had climbed Skiddaw by other than the main route from Keswick. Stan said the mountain was known as "Skidda" by local people. To Mrs Linton, already quoted, Skiddaw was "infinitely mild and paternal" with a "calm, grand front".

Bob reached for his Wainwright. AW (while acknowledging an absence of "frightful precipices" and "rugged outcrops") commended Skiddaw for its age (the oldest mountain in Lakeland judging by the evidence of its rocks) and for the way the lesser heights of the proud Skiddaw family provided an attractive buttress.

Ours had not been a difficult climb. Stan parked his car at a rakish angle in a by-road south of Bassenthwaite village, leaving a space a few feet wider than the titan of Lakeland roads, a cattle wagon. We walked through fields and then along the Edge, heading for Ullock Pike, which seen from this direction had been compared by Wainwright to "a young Matterhorn".

The route was much less boring than the direct approach from Keswick—a Long Drag to the summit of the fourth highest mountain in Lakeland.

We lingered on Ullock Pike for the view, knowing that at the summit of Skiddaw we would see little else but bits of slate, a triangulation station, several windbreaks and ramblers champing on ham sandwiches and Mars bars.

Now, couched in heather, we took in Bassenthwaite Lake (the only major stretch of water in Lakeland with "lake" in its title) at a sweeping glance. The atmosphere being clear, we looked across the northern plain to Solway and the blue hills of Galloway. We were ideally placed for viewing Derwentwater and the central fells.

Though Skiddaw blocked out the eastern sky, we had been conscious during the climb of the deeply glaciated Southerndale, with its sheep and ravens.

So to the summit, via Carlside Tarn and an unrelenting stony slope to the half mile long undulating ridge with its three "bumps", the most northern of which is the true summit of Skiddaw. Some visitors, lightly clad, were on a 50 mile circuit which would take in the three Lakeland peaks which have an elevation of over 3,000 ft., involving a total of 10,000 feet of climbing.

I carried a piece of the celebrated Skiddaw Slate, an ancient, crumbly rock of sedimentary origin, much older than the volcanics that overlie the slate beds in central Lakeland. This 450 million year old piece—a genuine antique!—was to be my contribution to the cairn.

There were grunts as I disturbed someone who was swaddling blistered feet in sticking plaster.

Keswick's mighty mountain not only provides a skyline feature from town but graces a million picture postcards, especially the view taking in Ashness Bridge, on the road to Watendlath. This is the most dramatic aspect. Back o' Skiddaw is a fairly shallow grassy slope forming part of a featureless basin which is the nursery of the Caldew.

The celebrities of the 19th century walked beside laden ponies. They were spared the travail of lugging rucksacks. On August 21, 1815, the Southeys of Keswick and the Wordsworths of Grasmere celebrated the victory at Waterloo by dancing round a bonfire, rolling balls of burning tow and generally desecrating the mountain top.

It is related that when the red-cloaked Wordsworth accidentally knocked over the container holding the water, the grog had to be drunk undiluted. An inebriated party returned to Keswick, with one one of the men flopping limply over the haunches of a pony.

Anyone who climbed Skiddaw must have a guide, of course. Harriet Martineau, who fancied herself as a guide book writer, mentioned the ease of ascent "even for ladies who have only to sit on their ponies to find themselves at the top after a ride of six miles". There must be a guide. "No kind of tourist should ever cross the higher passes or ascend the mountains without a guide".

There was time to visit the Little Man (2,837 ft), a mile from the Old Man. From here we made a bee-line to Sale How and Skiddaw House.

The cloud mass was breaking. Golden light spread over the northern fells.

We trudged to where Dash Beck becomes Whitewater Dash, tripping down a rock staircase, and Stan directed us unerringly to the car. We drove to the fleshpots of Keswick, which was visited by the 16th century topographer, William Camden, who found the place "in a fruitful field, encompass't with wet dewy mountains, and protected from the north-winds by that of Skiddaw . . ."

Esk Pike:
Storming the Bastion

WE WALKED by Sty Head and Sprinking Tarn to Esk Hause, at the hub of the Lakeland wheel. The Hause is arguably the wettest area in Lakeland. A bucket makes the best rain gauge.

It was raining at Seathwaite, at the head of Borrowdale. It is not always raining at Seathwaite. As the farmer says in a hoary old tale, "sometimes it snaws". Wordsworth observed that in Lakeland the rain comes down heartily and is frequently succeeded by clear, bright weather, "when every brook is vocal, and every torrent sonorous..."

The torrents we saw on the fellsides were white as milk. The voice of the beck had deepened to a roar. In dry spells, the river between Seathwaite and Seatoller withdraws to some mysterious subterranean course, but a few hours of heavy rain brings it back into turbulent view.

Seathwaite experiences climatic extremes. In summer I have seen it drought-stricken, as dusty as a desert, with the vegetation crunchy underfoot (as in 1983 and 1984) or half-drowned (as in 1985).

It was in 1985 that dalehead farmers who had normally cut grass for hay or conventional silage turned to what was then an unfamiliar technique—Big Bale Silage, mowing grass in the wet, having it machine-rolled into half-ton bales and enveloping them in black plastic bags to keep out the air. Each bag contained wet grass, a bit of mud—and a gallon or two of water!

The demand for plastic bags caused the price to rise from about £1 to nearly £2 each. A farmer lower down Borrowdale said grimly: "I reckon there'll be a gey lot o' plastic blowing aboot by spring".

As we passed Seathwaite Farm, we were almost bowled over by a cascade of newly-clipped Herdwick sheep looking for the nearest field and a further cascade of children who were darting from the life-saving cafe.

Occasionally, the yellow-painted Land Rovers of the local fell rescue team arrive at Seathwaite and ever-cheerful volunteers carrying specialist equipment head for the heights.

I used to have a "crack" with Joseph Cockburn, of Seatoller, who took part in rescue operations in the 1930s. They were organised by the St John's Ambulance Brigade and the stretcher was one of the rigid kind, with two poles and a canvas top. Also carried were wooden splints and bandages.

Joseph remarked: "Often we'd go up from the Borrowdale side, only to find that the Wasdale team had been called out as well. We'd meet on the tops. I've been in a party from Borrowdale who ended up in Wasdale—and we'd to walk back home. I'd get into bed as late as three o'clock..."

It was a good day on which to visit Esk Hause which, with a rainfall of about 185 inches per annum, is rarely dry underfoot. Seathwaite, presiding over the alluvial flats, shadowed by some of our shapeliest fells, has a just claim to being the wettest inhabited spot.

I had a "crack" with Stanley Edmondson, who was indeed clipping some sheep. Seathwaite is a place where there is non-stop variety. Even the dogs are perpetually occupied and, while waiting for sheep to be dipped or shorn or dosed, they use up their surplus nervous energy, running along the wall-tops.

We took the track for Stockley Bridge and Sty Head Tarn. Then it began to rain and I understood why the sheep-clippers of Seathwaite had not been relaxing until the quota for the day had been shorn.

The stones beneath our feet, polished by myriad boots, were slippery. The fast-moving clouds were mucky, as described to me by a small boy at a dalehead farm, where clouds were rarely any other colour but dark grey.

In the October of 1818, when Dorothy Wordsworth and "poor Miss Barker" went to Esk Hause, they took a cart from Miss Barker's house in Rosthwaite and left the cart at Seathwaite, proceeding on foot to Esk Hause. With them, as guide, was a shepherd who also carried the provisions.

In the event, the weather was so bright and settled, this trio went on to the summit of Scafell Pike. They "paused and kept silence to listen, and not a sound of any kind was to be heard".

We had our first "butty stop" near Sty Head, with our backs to the large first-aid box (it is big enough to take a stretcher). I recalled a story told to me by a retired waller who was familiar with Wasdale—of a man toiling up the Sty Head Pass from Wasdale who was over-taken by a "thunderplash" and got into the first-aid box for shelter. The box clicked shut and he found he could not push it open.

Hours later, he heard someone sitting on the box. What should he do? Shout—and cause the stranger to run away, fearing a ghost? Or simply lie there till he was too weak to do anything?

He spoke quietly, requesting that the box be opened. And it was—by an almost exhausted walker who was lost and dispirited. Each sav-ed the life of the other!

We now struck off towards Sprinkling Tarn. Two jet-black ravens were blown across the sky. Two lads on mountain bikes were blown to a standstill and had to walk for a while.

Colourful blobs on the lee sides of boulders by Sprinkling Tarn in-dicated where walkers had stopped to sup and eat. Their anoraks were merely blobs to me because by now my spectacles were rain-spattered and steamed-up.

And so we came to the slanting stretch of grassland known as Esk Hause, which might be termed the Crossroads of Mountain Lakeland—if only the paths crossed. Sitting at the Hause, I was aware only of walkers appearing from several directions, some being at the later stages of a climb to Scafell Pike, the attic of England.

E Lynn Linton (1864) mentioned "the famous Fludder's Brow where the guides and shepherds meet for business, as they do on High Street and used to do at the Justice Stone by Thirlmere".

There followed the dispiriting experience of eating tomato sand-wiches in the rain. We talked about the ancient traffic—axe-makers from Langdale, heading for the Plain where the axe heads would be completed and prepared for marketing; monastic parties en route for farms in Borrowdale and packhorse trains, the leading pony carrying a bell that jingled a warning to other track-users.

Wainwright indicated that the name Esk Hause was commonly (but incorrectly) used for the lower of the passes, "a much-trodden route", but should apply to the higher pass. The true Esk Hause (2,490 ft) is the head of Eskdale, a shallow depression between Esk Pike and Great End.

It was time to storm the bastions of Esk Pike (2,903 ft) and tick off another "Wainwright". To me, the Pike resembles a ruined castle, with a steep approach and the ancient walls reduced to a litter of great boulders. We crossed a grassy area—which became a parade ground in our fantasy world—before climbing the castle keep, which is the summit of the fell.

I rested part way up, to "admire the view", of course—and I picked out some of the tracks on the Hause. People were moving to the greater peaks—the Scafells—and also descending to Sty Head, to Borrowdale, to Langdale and into Eskdale.

Hause, from the old Norse, means a neck or pass. A compass is vital in a large open area which is confusing in mist. No fun is derived from descending into Langdale instead of Borrowdale.

Now our little party was aware of a brightening of the sky and of a parting of clouds. Shafts of light rested on features of the landscape. I could now clearly see a jaded tract of land, with Esk Hause in the foreground.

We returned to Seathwaite by Grain's Gill, where much of the path has been reinforced by skilfully laid stones placed side by side, tilting slightly to shed water. On our last visit, we crossed Seathwaite Fell, where rain gauges had been set, and made an ultra-steep descent to Stockley Bridge.

Now, walking carefully down the Gill, we had a gradual descent, with stones clinking underfoot, with the becks in spate and the ravens—those sacred birds of the Norsefolk—shaking water from their jet-black wings.

Dorothy Wordsworth and "poor Miss Baker" returned from Scafell Pike to Esk Hause and made the final descent to Seathwaite by starlight. "We travelled home in our Cart by Moonlight".

That day, they had every reason to be pleased with their "uncommon performances".

High Street:
Where Romans Tramped

BY JUPITER, but the breeze was "thin"! It came from the north-east. Bob, by his careful selection of the starting point, had at least contrived that it would be behind us. We would have wind-assistance on the long ridge walk to Racecourse Hill, alias High Street, a walk that climbs for over 2,600 feet among the eastern fells.

High Street is a name associated with the Romans who, having constructed some fine roads around the fells, now had to make their presence known among them. A party of Roman soldiers, setting out from the fort at Brocavum (Brougham), near tropical Penrith, would head with some foreboding for Galava (Ambleside).

This High Street is a long open stretch without pavements or shopping precinct. No Marks and Spencers nor British Home Stores is to be found here. At times, it is not easy to find the route.

Bob, Stan, Colin and I joined the line of the Roman road at Winder Hall Farm, Celleron. The ancient gods may have drawn a curtain of cloud across the sky, but no rain issued from it.

We had a dry path beneath our boots and a view south-westwards of the fells around the head of Ullswater as we followed what the Ordnance Survey map referred to as "ROMAN ROAD (course of)". The cartographers do well to qualify the name. It is certainly not the fine, flagged way a stranger would expect.

The Romans selected the line of an old British trackway, a route which for 12 continuous miles maintains a height of over 2,000 ft. They would therefore know the miseries of rain, mist and a wind chilly enough to put ice in their bloodstream.

Those imperial soldiers did not have to concern themselves with camping arrangements; they were quite capable of marching 25 (English) miles a day. The High Street route is just a long slog, demanding stamina, dedication, warm clothes and good boots.

Roman engineers, charged with linking Ambleside and Brougham, did not traverse a wilderness, especially on and around Moor Divock, to the north of the high hills, where the countryside had been benevolent enough to sustain a quite large Bronze Age population, judging by the number of cairns, stone circles and barrows [burial mounds].

A medieval document refers to High Street as Brethestrete—"the Briton's Road". Two thousand years before the Romans threw their weight about, this had possibly been one of the great trading routes, handling such items as the Cumbrian Stone Axe, made from volcanic rock located at the head of Great Langdale and in transit to customers all over the country.

As we got into our stride, I recalled highlights from my walking past. The first time I climbed High Street was from Haweswater with Dick Hilton, who had a wooden leg. We parked the car at the head of old Mardale, which Manchester Waterworks converted into Haweswater.

Wainwright lamented the loss of the old valley. Norman Nicholson, noting that the raised water level had flooded the intermediate land between the old lake and the fellside wrote of "great hills standing up to their waists in cold water".

The climb to Blea Water was enlivened by chirruping pipits. Blea Water looked dark blue. It is circular—a lakelet about which tales of mystery and intrigue might be written.The track led over slippery grass to the edge of Riggindale Crag at over 2,000 ft above sea level.

The valley that came into view looked simple in structure, bleak, its low areas near the stream holding a variety of hues, from rust to the bilious yellow-green of sphagnum. The beck had formed a series of stylish ox-bows. Black ponies gave to the austere valley an Icelandic touch. The side of Riggindale was a jumble of rocks, bilberry and small trees. Two cock ring ouzels had a skirmish. Other ouzels flew with chacking calls.

Now Dick had suffered grievous injuries while serving with the Army in Italy during the 1939-45 war. He had a wooden leg but a tremendous spirit which reduced problems to minor concerns. As we strode up the fellside, I heard the rhythmic thwack, plonk, of boot and artificial limb.

Then there was the morning when I looked at High Street from Kidsty Pike, across the glaciated valley of Riggindale. As I looked, and champed a sandwich, one of the local eagles appeared, riding on an updraught.

We stared at each other from a range of no more than 50 yards. That adult golden eagle belonged to the only nesting pair in England. The bird continued to glide, making subtle adjustments to the trim of wings and tail, until it became a dark speck in a summer-blue sky.

Another day, from Riggindale itself, I looked up on hearing the honk of a carrion crow and saw this bird was tailing an eagle. A peregrine falcon took over the harassment and in due course two eagles and two falcons were in the same limited space and the air held the excited chatter of the smaller birds.

Now four walking friends were heading for High Street the long but easy way. We had "musical accompaniment" from singing larks. A bird would rise like a feathered helicopter to fill the air with cascades of sweet notes.

Fell ponies, some brown, some black, had foals at foot. Twenty or more of these stocky, good-natured, semi-wild ponies were scattered about the grassy hills. It is not unlikely that the Romans used ponies of this type as pack animals or to carry material to where they were building forts.

The fell ponies champing coarse grasses at the approach to High Street belonged to farmers at Bampton and Butterwick, Helton and Askham—settlements in the valley of the Lowther. Ponies share the high grazings with sheep and red deer.

These ponies, untouched by human hand for the first few years of their lives, drop their foals on lower ground. This is also the time when the stallion set the seeds for another generation of ponies. Though hardy animals, fell ponies tend to fall back into Heltondale during the leanest part of the winter. Farmers provide them with supplementary feed.

Lines of puzzlement appeared on the foreheads of Stan and Bob as they tried to find sections of High Street which had been reduced to a porridge-like mush by ramblers' feet and the sharp cleaves of sheep.

We decided that High Street is easy to find, if you know precisely where it is! There is but one moorland signpost, where tracks cross.

I looked for the marks of a Roman chariot (it was too much to expect the imprint of a sandalled foot) but there were only the tracks made by the bell-shaped feet of ponies and the ubiquitous sheep. In the end, we trusted to the map-reading of mountain-bikists.

Bob's stomach told him it was butty-time and so we headed for a glamorous eating-place—two concentric stone circles, where we could also dream about Ancient Brits. Instead, a chilling wind kept us moving. We delayed eating our packed meals until we reached a small stone enclosure on our way to Bonscale Pike.

Now there was heather and bracken underfoot. Where there is heather, there should be grouse, reasoned Stan, but although we looked hard the best evidence of "moorcock" was a row of old grouse butts, each composed of two stakes driven into the ground, with a screen of vegetation behind which the marksman could hide.

A slight diversion took us to Arthur's Pike and Bonscale Pike, each having its major cairn and some subsidiary cairns at points where the views were truly panoramic. The map showed a reservoir, which presumably regulated the flow of water to some settlement by the lake.

Was it Ulf, a Norse settler, whose name is associated with serpentine Ullswater? Or, as one commentator has claimed, could the name be a pleonasm, the prefix meaning water—el, hel, ul, hul, etc., all the same thing—and therefore "water-water"?

Bob preferred the tea-tea theory and pronounced that viewpoint for Ullswater as a re-fuelling station.

The lake was filling up with yachts and from the heights they resembled multi-toned water beetles. We watched the graceful steamers as they operated between Glenridding, Howtown and Pooley Bridge.

Then it was time to rejoin the Roman Road and in due course to leave it to cross the vast dome of Loadpot Hill, on the skirts of which were yet more fell ponies, plus a kestrel, seen hovering against the powder-blue sky. A snipe rose from a marshy spot with an alarm cry like a sneeze.

Just south of Loadspot, a visitor with three small spaniels sat on a heap of well-masoned stones as though on a monstrous seat; he was actually using what remains of the chimney of an old shooting lodge

71

of the Lonsdales which had the grand name of Lowther House. There were adjacent stables for the ponies that bore the sportsmen to the heights and also carried food and liquid refreshment.

The Roman Road continued to unfold in long stretches, going by Wether Hill, Red Crag, Raven Howe and High Raise, where a black dot against a cloud is always worthy of a second glance. It might be one of the few Lakeland golden eagles.

So to the summit plateau of High Street, at an elevation of 2,717 ft, a grassy top as the sequence to a walk on a grassy ridge. At least the ground was cushioned for almost all the way.

Racecourse Hill (a half-forgotten name for High Street) was (until about 1835) a setting for the Shepherds' Meet, where stray herdwicks were restored to their rightful owners and an excuse was found for sports and merriment. The horse-racing took place in high summer. Wrestlers of the Cumberland and Westmorland style gathered to match their skills and stamina against each other.

A Victorian guidebook mentions the annual meeting held on the summit by the shepherds of Patterdale, Martindale, Mardale, Kentmere and Troutbeck, "when racing and various games took place as at a fair, and refreshments were brought from the neighbouring villages. . .It is comparatively little visited by the majority of lake tourists because of its distance from those inns where they can be comfortably housed".

The rewards for the climb to the plateau is now, as then, "scenes of the most fantastic, wild and picturesque beauty". Each of us had our memories. For me, it was of Dick Hilton and the alternative thwack and clump of boot and wooden leg on the long, hard track.

Caw Fell:
Over the Big Red Wall

IT WAS time, said Bob, to tick off some of the Wainwrights near Ennerdale Lake. The other members of our informal group did not demur. We made for what Wainwright described as "rolling grasslands linking the untamed heights with the cultivated valleys" and "scenery that has not changed since the world began".

We were on vast upland grazings where almost every creature that moves is a sheep. Habitations are few and far apart. Yet to judge by prehistoric remains, it was a well-populated area several thousand years ago.

We parked near one of the antiquities—the Kinniside Stone Circle. It was fun to try and imagine the religious ceremonies or social occasions which drew people to this prominent place. Down at Ennerdale Bridge, a man laughed and said the circle was a Victorian spoof.

We passed through a gate, symbol of privacy, into an area smothered by sitka spruce and a few larches. Wordsworth described the new-fangled larch plantations of his day as "vegetable manufactory". What would he have written about the new upland forests?

Our route was an old ironstone mine track through the sheep ranges of Kinniside. Mile after mile, there was no human dwelling to be seen. When sheep are gathered in these parts, those at the northern (National Trust) end are driven down to Swinside for sorting.

At the other end of the fell (where farmers have joined together in a Graziers' Society), the sheep stocks converge at the pens near Friars' Bridge.

Where track and trees petered out, the Big Red Wall begins its tall, drystone course, extending across the landscape like some latter-day Hadrian's Wall, minus the fortlets. The reddish appearance of the wall is from a local granite.

When we first ventured this way, a stretch of two and a-half miles of wall was being restored by skilled workers who had music while they worked, judging from the battery-operated radio which lay beneath an upturned plastic bucket, awaiting their next spell of duty.

The National Trust acquired the land and a badly-gapped wall from the Leconfield Estate. At one time, it seemed that a wire fence would be made to divide up the sheep ranges. Happily, some funds and labour were found to "do t'job reight". They were busy on the first phase of its restoration, from about where we stood to a place with the unLakelandish name of Cosy Corner.

The Trust owns the land north of the wall; it goes with Mireside Farm. South of the wall is a "stinted" common where farmers banded themselves together as the afforementioned Graziers' Society. A "stint" is a unit of pasturage, representing what would be needed by a sheep.

In such a bleak area, with outcropping rock and varying types of ground, acres have little relevance to the stock-carrying capacity. More than one stint is required to graze a cow or a horse. The farmers recognise the folly of exceeding the quota. Before the Big Red Wall was repaired, there had been endless discussions about sheep leaving their "heafs" to graze in others.

For generations, the farmers and their men took stray sheep to Cosy Corner, where they had their "letterbox", a cavity in which notes relating to any strays were left. A lady who lived up the valley when it held the huge farm of Gillithwaite described the cavity on the fellside as "a sort of shepherds' postbox".

The warden, Jim Loxham, whom we met up by the Big Red Wall, deduced that most of these felltop walls were built in the late 18th and early 19th centuries. The Kinniside Wall is marked on a map of 1820. Jim told me that the wall is five or six miles long in its entirety.

Beyond Iron Crag, it follows a flank of Caw Fell and the watershed over Gowder Crag before running over Haycock and on to end abruptly at the crags of Great Scoat Fell, above the col separating this fell from Pillar.

As a stock barrier, the Big Red Wall had become ineffective, and when manpower and funds were available, rather than replace it with posts and wire it was decided to restore it as a drystone wall. It

74

was done systematically. The map was consulted and the line of the wall divided into 100-metre sections, over each of which was written the estimated number of "man days" it would take to complete it.

Wainwright's guide led us to Caw Fell and Silver Cove, thence down the heathery fellside to The Side.

It was a day of slack air, when gulls flying low over Ennerdale could admire their reflections in the water. Dull light gave a sense of mystery to Side Wood, which is seen by Wainwright fans who follow the Coast to Coast Walk.

Lakeland, some 300 years ago, was the most wooded area of Britain and it still abounds in little patches of what is essentially primary woodland, where there has never been anything on the site apart from trees. Deforestation was rapid in the Middle Ages when native woodland provided timber for charcoal production to feed the bloomeries where iron was produced. The presence of a bloomery across the lake was to be recalled in the name of the watercourse— Smithy Beck.

Jim Loxham was of the opinon that about two centuries had passed since Side Wood was last coppiced. He had found three "steadings" or charcoal pits, one being complete with a low stone wall built to hold the steeple-like roof of birch and thatch under which the charcoal-burners lived for weeks on end in summer while tending the charcoal "burn".

Ennerdale Water offered a mirror image of the tree-lined shores. Herdwicks stared hopefully towards a party of Coast to Coast walkers, hoping to augment their diet of fescue grass with sand-wiches.

Said Jim: "You get the long distance walk-baggers. You get people who have not walked in their lives before. It seemed like a good idea at the time. Then you get people who are just out for enjoyment. Some do it in small bites, over a number of week-ends. Others are run-ning it. Some take a fortnight over it. Others use it as a pub-crawl. There are all sorts of reasons for doing it".

The Freshwater Biological Association used to send men to Enner-dale Lake to collect specimens of a rare shrimp, mysis relicta. This was originally a saltwater shrimp which had to change its life-style when Ennerdale, a fjord in remote times, was cut off from the sea by geological changes.

A square canvas boat was kept at the old Anglers' Inn. Preparing it for a voyage was almost as complex as erecting a deck chair. "You had to stand up and row it. You couldn't row against the wind. On a windy day you might get blown down to the dam".

Side Wood, a nesting place for redstart and pied flycatcher, has a special importance to naturalists because of the type of vegetation it contains—a type found only on the Atlantic seaboard of Europe and, in particular, mosses and lichens which thrive where sheep graze in reasonable numbers, limiting the growth of much of the under-vegetation that would otherwise shade out the rare plants.

Jim referred to "a difficult balancing act. Too little grazing and we lose some of the liverworts, lichens and mosses. Too much grazing, and the wood cannot regenerate itself".

In the wood was birch, which is invasive, colonising quickly. This useful pioneer tree species shelters other emergent species and eventually is crowded out by oak. There is rather more of the sessile oak in the eastern end than the west. The low shrub canopy includes hazel and holly, with ash trees growing on the flushes.

Side Wood is on a giant scree, with ankle-wrenching assemblies of boulders. Soon we were standing in a pleasant little glade, where the ground was level and the vegetation low and even. This was man-made, one of the trio of charcoal-steadings to which I have already referred. All the components are there—woodland, flowing water, the platform for the burn and what remains of the wigwam-like shelter for the burners.

In our walk we had descended from the high montane to a mixed woodland in a mile or two. The lushness of the vegetation was in part due to the repair work on the Big Red Wall.

Binsey:
Where the Wind is at Home

BINSEY is the odd man out. AW compared its detached, solitary state with a dunce, made to stand in a corner. Whenever Bob wanted to stimulate me to weekday walking on my own, he would say: "Go and do Binsey. It's a quiet stroll".

In fact, it was during some mopping up of awkwardly-placed little peaks that we parked the car near Binsey Lodge and negotiated some metal gates at a gathering place for sheep to find ourselves on a path that ascended smoothly into the mist.

Bob, consulting Wainwright, informed me that Binsey is composed of volcanic rock, not slate like its big neighbours. And I told Bob about the first time a Lakelander had mentioned Binsey to me: and that was William Wilson, who lived at Herdwick View, near where Bassenthwaite Lake outflows and, besotted by the herdwick breed, had some stained glass images of sheep set in the sitting room window.

It is no wonder that his many friends referred to him as Herdwick Billy. After years of farming at Watendlath and in the Newlands Valley, he moved to Bassenthwaite in 1932, but ran some herdwicks on Binsey where (it seems) their descendants still live.

There is little to relate of our ascent of Binsey. We put one foot before the other on a route on which a vehicle had wiped its feet but which had not lost its coverlet of green.

We came under the gaze of herdwicks and Swaledales and crosses between the two breeds. They stared at us with eyes as ancient looking as the stones about them.

The mist enveloped us. We kept going uphill, confident it would lead us to the summit, and so it did. Binsey had sheltered us from the wind. Within a few paces of the top, we met the savage blast of a north-westerly. It was an effort to reach the cairn. Before my eyes watered in the cold air, I saw the summit was pitted as though with craters. They were basin-like depressions in the boulderfield—primitive windcheaters made by earlier visitors.

AW sketched himself, with tousled hair, beefy frame and trousers held up by braces, sitting on one of the heaps of stones. The caption to this drawing was: "Prehistoric tumulus and Ancient Briton".

In summer, the purple heather delights. And up here are splendid views of the northern fells. In the other direction is the gleam of sunlight on the Solway and, beyond—the blue hills of Scotland.

Glaramara:

Tongue of Borrowdale

TO THE Norse settlers, the fell was Glaeframerhi (a reference to its "chasms" and situation as a boundary marker). The name became corrupted over the years into Glaramara, the present delightful title. The boundary referred to may have been that of land bought by the Abbots of Furness early in the 13th century.

Glaramara (2,560 feet) is the name of a feature on an isolated mass of fell country twixt Grains Gill and Langstrath that seemed to early visitors to block Borrowdale, hence its nickname of the "tongue" of Borrowdale. Hugh Walpole, creator of the Herries Chronicles, associated Glaramara with some of the fictitious adventures.

Glaramara, the 42nd name in the list of the highest fells, is often regarded as an intermediate fell—a stopping place en route between what are thought of as nobler peaks. Yet Wainwright, a perceptive man, recognised the worthiness of Glaramara, remarking that although overtopped by many fells, this fell is overshadowed by none.

The most popular ascent from Borrowdale begins opposite Mountain View, near Seatoller, and proceeds by way of Thorneythwaite Fell and a line west of Raven Crag and Combe Head to Glaramara, continuing to Allen Crag and returning to the dale under the vast face of Great End and Stockley Bridge.

Bob chose to start at Stonethwaite, in a side valley of Borrowdale. Glaramara, steep and rough, is a fell to be stormed. The view of this secluded village from the main road takes in the stately dome of Eagle Crag.

We four followed the tarmac until it became a path and we used that path to a gate which provided an entry into the wooded area beside Little Stanger Gill.

Such gashes on the steep fellsides are the last refuge of native trees and plants, though we strode under a canopy of oak trees and admired the purple spire of the foxglove, which is certainly not on the endangered list.

Using a platform of rock, we looked out towards Rosthwaite, with the bountifully-wooded hills of Borrowdale in clear view. We continued up the steep gill, and emerged from tree cover to be dazzled by the brilliance of the June sunlight. We had our butty-stop and then dozed off in the hot sunshine.

On these lone heights, parsley fern was profuse and common butterwort was ready to trap with its stickiness any wayward insect.

Now Derwentwater was in view and, beyond, Skiddaw. We were climbing Bessyboot—the northern extremity of Rosthwaite Fell. Bilberry was common. Pools held flowering bogbean. A small dark butterfly was surely the mountain ringlet.

We were on nodding terms with Green and Great Gable. There were to be several false summits before we attained the true one at 2,572 ft. Here was an expanse of coarse grasses with outcropping rocks. From here we had a splendid view of the Langdale Pikes from an unusual angle, the cone of Pike o'Stickle giving a distinctive appearance to the undulations of a grassy landscape.

Up here is Hind Side (west) on which there were no female red deer and Buzzard Knott (east) which no longer appears to attract buzzards.

On to Allen Crags and Esk Hause, where major paths meet. Thence by Seathwaite Fell, with a toe-achingly steep descent to Seathwaite. For the first time in my life, I was desperate to protect my skin from the scorching heat.

It was with rapture that we visited the small cafe at Seathwaite to revel in chilled drinks.

Helvellyn:
Friendly Giant

IT WAS Wainwright who described Helvellyn as "a very friendly giant". He had commented on its lovely name and lofty altitude. He observed what others have noted, that there is a great difference in appeal between the plain western side and the indented east.

We did not emulate Canon Rawnsley in ascending Helvellyn in semi-darkness and staying on its summit to witness the sunrise. Rawnsley penned a piece which really should be recited to music:

"Then, as we watched, making all the landscape darker for his advent, we saw above Crossfell a ruby jewel burn—a jewel first in lozenge shape that grew to semicircle, and at last, almost as it seemed with a bound, leapt up a perfect disk above the hills".

We climbed on to Nethermost Pike from Grisedale and then walked the ridge to find the summit (3,116 ft) in mist as thick as a dish-clout, as they used to say in the industrial towns.

We did not climb alone, Helvellyn being justifiably popular because of the ease of access and its central position in the scheme of things. It's a dangerous spot, of course. A Victorian visitor found the path "shockingly bad" and not far from the summit was made suddenly aware of a "terrible precipice with a lake at the bottom, not ten yards away. Now really, don't you think a railing ought to be put up in a place like that?"

The differences between the western and eastern sides of Helvellyn are astonishing. Steep-sided in the west, in the east it was a playground of glacial ice, which deeply gouged the rocks, creating hanging valleys and thin ridges—Swirrel Edge and Striding Edge—which have become thinner still through weathering.

Two combs hold tarns which catch the light and are like the eyes of the mountain.

We ascended Helvellyn almost sixty years after two men "bagged" the peak using an aircraft. Michael Berry had been keen to celebrate the anniversary of the arrival of an aircraft on December 22, 1926. The pilot and his companion were John Leeming, chairman of the Lancashire Aero Club and Bert Hinkler, the chief test pilot for A V Roe and Company.

The attempt to put an aircraft down on Helvellyn took place in secret, a previous attempt having failed through poor visibility. Flying from a field at Lancaster in a single-engined Avro 585 Gosport, which had not yet been awarded its certificate of air worthiness, the two men passed over Scafell and located their destination, though it was partly obscured by cloud banks.

These were less alarming than the "air pockets". The plane was tossed about like a cork in the sea. In one slack area, the aircraft fell like a stone for 500 feet before control was regained. Hinkler, lifted clear of his seat, lost the cushion on which he had been sitting when it blew away.

On that outward journey, having fuel blockage problems, Leeming was forced to land his aircraft in Calgarth Park, where the children of the Ethel Hedley Memorial Hospital, in a fever of anticipation about Christmas, thought that Santa Claus was about to visit them.

Ten minutes after taking off, the aircraft had touched down on Helvellyn. The solitary witness to the landing was a bemused Professor of Greek who was visiting the area on holiday. He was able to confirm the time of landing, 1.35 pm. The aeronauts took off after being on Helvellyn for 20 minutes. A plaque commemorates their achievement.

That day, we left Helvellyn by Swirral Edge and Catstycam. On the next occasion, we ventured north of Helvellyn on to the grassy Dodds where, in contrast, hardly anyone was seen. We walked 13½ miles, ascending a total of some 3,000 ft., which is nothing special by Joss Naylor standards but commendable for an ageing dodderer like me.

We began at Dockray, gaining elevation gently, beside a long wall which flanked the "brown" hills. Our eyes strayed frequently from the path to take in the head of Ullswater, where the fells leap straight from the water like mountains from fjords in Norway and where clouds swirl about them like steam from a cauldron.

We ascended to Glencoynedale where, at a stand of gale-weary pines, we turned abruptly west. The first butty-stop was within the crumbling walls of a sheepfold, from which a fox made its escape at full speed.

Not being able to make a bee-line for Stybarrow Dodd, we went for Green Side, using a narrow path which was more suited to sheep than humans. Later, at the south-western cairn of Stybarrow Dodd, we let our eyes wander slowly over the Thirlmere area.

Here, to the north of Helvellyn, which would be teeming with people, we strolled comfortably on grassy terrain which, for most of the time, we had to ourselves. There was easy ground to Watson's Dodd, thence to great Dodd at 2,807 ft.

Our last summit of the day was Clough Head, from which we looked over Threlkeld and Keswick. In view directly ahead were Skiddaw and Blencathra. There was a gleam on Bassenthwaite Lake. Far off to the east was the blue-grey procession of Pennine peaks.

We resisted the temptation to make an immediate descent but carried on to White Pike, thence to the old coach road. Others were proposing to follow it back to Dockray. We had a second car stationed in the Vale of St John.

The old coach route and old quarry trackbeds led us back to the car. We had the sun in our faces and enough tea in the thermos flasks to provide us with a third butty-stop.

Pillar and the Black Sail Pass

THREE major dales—Wasdale, Ennerdale and Eskdale—begin among the gaunt western fells but open their mouths to mild breezes sweeping in from the Cumbrian Sea.

The mountains may be dour and chilly, but the dales from which they appear to spring are near to sea level. When a wind makes snow-castles on the fells, the dales are strips of verdant green.

At Wasdale Head, the fells usually block out two-thirds of the sky. This day, they had been softened by mist and did not look quite so formidable.

We four entered one of the recesses of Lakeland which, until the "touroids" arrived about a century ago, housed a lost race of almost pure Vikings. It was an exceedingly noisy place for 83 years until 1890, when Will Ritson, who had been mine host at the local inn, breathed his last.

Will was of statesman stock—yan of us! He claimed for himself the title of Biggest Liar, though in a softer moment he confessed: "The lies Ah tell isn't malicious; they're nobbut gert big exaggerations". Will took a bishop to the summit of Scafell Pike and said: "Here you are, Mr Bishop: as near heaven as ye ever will be".

At one time, the dead of Wasdale were borne on horseback to St Catherine's Church at Boot, in Eskdale, for burial. It is said that a horse bearing the body of a young man took fright, bolted and could not be traced in the mist. The bereaved mother fretted over the double loss of her son, and she died. When the funeral procession was crossing into Eskdale, the horse carrying her coffin bolted and was not seen again—except as an apparition.

Visiting the head of Wasdale is like returning to the Stone Age. Everywhere there are heaps of stones, washed down in ancient times from what are now among Lakeland's shapeliest fells. The fells themselves have a careworn appearance from their fan-shaped screes. Dull red screes characterise Gable, the centrepiece of Wasdale's mountain showcase.

Walls are not uncommon in Lakeland as a whole but at Wasdale Head they seem more substantial, more numerous than anywhere else. They jostle round the farmhouses; they extend across the level ground and then head across the lower fells, enclosing the big pastures.

The wallscapes of Wasdale impress every visitor. Early walls were fashioned by those who were simply clearing the ground of the litter of boulders left by Pleistocene ice.

William Monkhouse, a retired shepherd, who returns periodically to the dale where he worked for many years, told me in his delightful Cumbrian speech: "It wad be nice if one o' them auld chaps come back to tell us about t'walls." William also enthused about the remote crofts, "lile spots where sheep can shelter".

We were chatting in the kitchen of Scott Naylor's farmhouse. William mentioned some large boulders which provide bield, or shelter, for sheep. "There's a big rock yonder: you can see it when you get to t'door. Eight or ten sheep can get under yon rock and they'd be as dry in a storm as if they were sheltering in this house."

His quick eyes took in other features of the fell. "A little bit further on, there's a nice round sheepfold: them auld chaps built that up. Once when we went to t'fell we found a gap in it. I said: 'them auld chaps walled this. I mustn't let it spoil. I can easy put this gap up.' I did—and I don't think there's bin a gap in that wall since".

The Wasdale stones, trundled along by wind or beck, long since lost their large size and keen edges. "I reckon we could do wi' taking some sandpaper to 'em to help make 'em stick," said William.

The weather causes most of the damage to the walls. Freeze-thaw conditions, the weight of stone, softening and shifting of the ground and, in Wasdale, a high wind funnelled by the fells, all weaken the ancient boundaries. A farmer's wife told me that the east wind descends like a demon on the head of the fell, stripping slates from roofs and battering the walls.

Our excursion to Pillar began with a drink at a modernised hotel and a stroll in the company of Mosedale Beck. There followed a climb so steep that I even saw flies resting!

Bob was not able to organise a "sudden death" approach to Pillar, for as Edward Baines wrote: "At the head of the valley soars the almost inaccessible Pillar". Bob therefore arranged for a circuit, keeping the popular High Level Route and Black Sail Pass to the last.

The steepness of the ascent from Mosedale to Dore Head was undoubtedly classifiable as a "red mist job". We clawed our way upwards for well over 1,000 ft. The reward was a view through swirling mist of Wastwater and its Screes.

At Red Pike, Colin was coaxed into occupying The Chair, a distinctive cairn with seating space and arm rests, for the benefit of Bob's camera. This peak, at 2,707 ft, would in any other location be venerated. At Wasdale, it has too much competition.

We walked amid scenes of increasing grandeur. The landforms were dark—dull, indeed—in the mist, but when we were able to find tattered edges of the cloying vapour we had windows on Lakeland at its most dramatic.

We arrived at the little-known Scoat Fell and moved along an airy ridge to visit the famous and shapely Steeple, which is in effect just a pointed rock. On our way to its constricted summit, we avoided looking down on either side while we were actually moving. From Steeple, the land slips away into Ennerdale. Having attained the roof of the district, we could with little extra effort go to Pillar.

The mist cleared long enough for us to see Scafell Pike, which from an elevation point of view, is King of the Cumbrian Fells. Also in clear view was the Young Pretender—Great Gable. Pillar was named after Pillar Rock, a monstrous mass of vertical crag, and so we looked down from Robinson's Cairn to where the Rock seemed to be poised ready to crash down on to Ennerdale, though it is unlikely to move an inch in our time.

To Jonathan Otley, the writer of an early guide book to the Lakes (1825), Pillar Rock was "unclimbable". In the following year, it was climbed by a local man, John Atkinson.

The first ascent by an off-comer [someone not of the immediate area] was by Lieut Wilson, a naval officer who lived at Troutbeck. He jotted down details of his climb, slipped them into a ginger beer bottle and stuck the bottle in a cairn.

The deeds of early climbers have not been forgotten. Local people still talk with awe of the experiences of a parson, James "Steeple" Jackson, who was so proud of his achievements in this area he called himself "Patriarch of the Pillarites". His nickname of Steeple had no connection with the mountain of that name, but was derived from a spell of Do-it-Yourself when masons refused to carry out repairs to his church steeple.

Jackson and a friend surmounted Pillar Rock in 1875, when the parson was 79 years old. The principal items of equipment were a rope, spike-nails and a hammer!

We were content, like spectators at the centenary of the first ascent, in 1926, to occupy suitable fellside ledges, "perched like so many sea-birds on their cliffs", and watch the action.

Eastwards we walked, on the low path to Looking Stead (2,058 ft), the dispersal of large boulders determining where the path would go and then we crossed over Black Sail Pass and were back in Mosedale, with Wasdale Head not far away.

Gowbarrow Park and Aira Force

THE Lakeland fells gleamed with new snow—though not enough snow to clog the fine detail. Bob announced a high ridge walk between Hartsop and Troutbeck, with the prospect of bagging no less than three Wainwrights on the way. We would walk with a northwest wind and snow showers at our backs, not in our faces.

The fells looked like iced wedding cakes in a shop window. The sky was not exactly cloudless but the clouds were small, white and innocuous. Sunshine brought out the coppery tone of bracken on the lower fellsides and accentuated the fresh green of the dale fields.

Leaving Stan's car at Troutbeck, we motored northwards in my vehicle, beginning with a countryside which had a hint of springtime about it and within minutes experiencing the wintry chill of a snowblown Kirkstone Pass.

Here the anticipated north-west wind had picked up fresh snow from the fells and deposited a wall-to-wall carpet of glistening whiteness on the road. There was not enough salt on the road to flavour a bag of potato crisps, much less melt the skiddy surface.

Beyond the inn, where the road began to dip towards Brotherswater and Hartsop, conditions were so treacherous that traffic was moving downhill at one or two miles an hour, if it moved at all. Cars coming up the hill came to a halt with spinning wheels.

A southbound car passed us with roar of engine and whine of tyres against ice, while two young men sitting on the front of the bonnet encouraged the tyres to grip with some spectacular bouncing. Opportunist Bob recorded the incidents on film.

With much time lost, and the possibility of chaos on Kirkstone for hours to come, Bob announced Plan 2, which was to explore wedge-shaped Gowbarrow Fell, a popular haunt of picnic parties which has also been called "a mountain park", retaining something of the wilderness flavour for those who are prepared to walk more than half a mile from the car park. It also incorporates Aira Force, a Lakeland honeypot.

Ullswater was choppy and chilling, like an inland sea. Buzzards circled over the scrag-ends of old woods on its shore. On this February day, when the weather forecasters had pronounced that more snow was to be expected, the car park was almost full and the nearest snow was falling on the Grampians.

Having equipped ourselves for combat with the expected "snow-dogs", I felt a little self-conscious—over-dressed indeed—as we clomped along the start of the path that fringes the higher parts of Gowbarrow Park. A small girl beheld our passing with drooping lower jaws, as though she was witnessing space-invaders. I was glad that Bob had not insisted on taking ice-axes.

The path climbed to the classic view of the head of Ullswater with its bays and promontories, its woods and high fells. Far below, standing out against the green flats was the enigmatic building with an almost unpronounceable name—Lyulph's Tower, derived ('tis said) from L'ulf, the first Lord of Ullswater.

E Lynn Linton, the Victorian novelist, described the tower as "a mere modern make-believe, with glazed windows among the ivy and cucumber frames at the tops of the towers". She added that the views from it were fine and it had a pair or two of antlers worth seeing.

Early last century, the Duke of Norfolk used an old tower as a shooting lodge. Gowbarrow was then a deer park with a high restraining wall. Mrs Linton mentioned the joy of visiting the fell and naming the surrounding mountains one by one. "And when you are there, a few deer will probably come about you and stand and gaze, much as they might have done when a Norman baron hunted them with sound of horn and twang of bow, and a villein's life was held of less importance than theirs".

It was an ostentatious age, hence the transformation of an old tower into something that would appeal to Walter Scott or Queen Victoria—a romantic building as its name implies. We saw it on a morning when there was a suitably romantic backdrop—a lake sheened with silver light backed by lofty fells that looked mysterious in shadow.

Bob's eyes misted over. Just as I thought he was about to leap on to a rock and recite a sonnet, he pointed to a lichened stone seat set against a lichened stone crag and pronounced it was time for a butty-stop.

Could there be a finer situation for a snack (granted good weather) than this memorial seat, overlooking a cairned knoll known as Yew Crag with, beyond, the snow-dusted form of Hallin Fell?

So far, we had not been tested by either the weather or the terrain. Winter was awaiting us round the corner. We turned northwards, with our feet crunching on an inch or two of snow and a view of snow and wizened grasses.

On Gowbarrow, the paths are as indispensable as are tracks to a train. The alternative to a path is a struggle through rank heather, whippy grass and knobbly rocks. The main path takes its time to reach the summit, which is certainly not the first high knob of ground to come into view, a knob which is inappropriately called Green Hill.

With Stan in the lead, we gained elevation, until we had a buzzard's eye view of a straddle of trees and rough grasses extending to where, on the lake shore, a trickle of cars was moving in defiance of the woeful tidings of the morning's weather forecast.

The views continued to enchant us, especially when framed by some of the large ash trees which had rooted in the crags. The path wandered off to Swinburn's Park. We bore to the left, moving uphill, braving the worst of the wind at the summit where a triangulation station stood looking like some altar to an earth-god. It was now being used to hold the medallion of the National Trust. Bob could only recall one other trig. point so bedecked and that is on Black Fell, near Tarn Hows.

We descended to Ulcat Row and turned homeward, using another terrace-like path round the lower slopes of Gowbarrow. Soon we heard the sharp, clear voice of Riddings Beck, which had gone white with fury as it encountered boulders and tree roots on its way to Ullswater via Aira Force.

The trees included some old warriors which had lived long enough to become characters and, in this humid area, had gathered much moss, from which sprouted a variety of plants, including foxglove. It was like being in a temperate-zone rain forest.

So to High Force, spurting into the gorge before using a rock staircase to a pool far below. The humidity was high. Those wearing spectacles had them finely speckled with moisture. I was reminded of the old dalesman's comment when someone was bragging about a waterfall: "There's nowt to stop it!"

Two bridges were ideal viewing places—the topmost bridge conventional, the lower bridge consisting of near vertical pieces of slate which were held together simply by the pressure of one stone against another. There was not a dab of mortar in sight.

The beckside path led us back to the car park, toilet block and cafe. In quieter times, Dorothy and William Wordsworth, walking where Aira Force gives Ullswater a transfusion of cold water, were moved by the sight of breeze-tossed daffodils in this lightly wooded area by the lake.

Wild daffodils flowering beside Ullswater were written about by Dorothy in her journal. William, who was to write a soppy story about Aira Force, saw the daffodil notes, lifted them, versified them, added some profundities and gave us something which (unlike the tear-jerking tale of Aira Force) is worth remembering.

Stan pronounced our tour of snowbound Gowbarrow an excellent walk. The modern visitor to Aira Force tends to use an uncouth word like "gob-smacked". Mrs Linton put it more tenderly when she described this wooded gill as "a place for all time and for all ages, for all moods and for all minds".

Bob began to speak. Could it be that we were about to be given a Wordsworthian recital, including that poem about daffodils?

Bob simply observed: "Right, lads—it's time for toilets and tea!"

The Wainwright Gate

ONE Wainwright fan who likes a touch of whimsy, makes a point of using one of the few remaining iron gates, hanging from a substantial stoop, but serving no useful purpose because the wires of the supporting fence long since rusted away.

He calls such a structure "a Wainwright gate" because AW made a point of mentioning one.

Wainwright was fascinated by gates. Like him, they are individualistic. "There seems as many ways of fastening a gate as there are gates...No two are quite alike".

Lingmoor Fell:
Marts and Whisky

WE ARRIVED early enough at Elterwater to find a space in the official parking area. We warmed up our boots during the walk to Baysbrown, at the foot of Lingmoor.

I mentioned the chats I had with Frank Birkett, whose home (overlooking the common at Elterwater) appeared to have no bedroom windows. In fact, these are at the sides. A young architect commissioned by Frank and his new wife, in days long gone, attempted to give this house the appearance of an agricultural outbuilding.

I had many a "crack" with the Birketts on winter days, being warmed within by hot tea and without by direct heat from a coal fire. Now, with Bob, I was following a path through the woods that Frank and I had taken when he told me of local quarries and charcoal-burning.

We were in a world of "pinking" chaffinches and "mewing buzzards" with a canopy of deciduous trees between us and a clear sky.

Frank had a fund of tales, including that of the drunken man who while walking home after drinking at Elterwater, and reaching a point where a five-barred gate was situated, put out a hand which, alas, passed cleanly between two bars. The walker bumped his nose on the woodwork!

One of Frank's favourite topics was Lanty Slee, a ubiquitous whisky distiller who had as many "secret" caves in the Lake District as there are Bonnie Prince Charlie caves in Scotland.

Frank's father met Lanty one night in the woodland near Baysbrown. Lanty was carrying a sample of his latest distillation and he offered father a sip. "It was grand stuff an' all", I was told.

Bob and I crossed the line of an old bridleway connecting "Gurt" Langdale with "Lile" Langdale. I re-located a feature which Frank

93

had found for me—the substantial stone base of what had been a shed built for a diesel engine, which provided power for Moss Shed Quarry.

Wainwright wrote of the "varied attractions" of Lingmoor. It had not only nurtured sheep but provided a plentiful supply of durable green stone. The quarries pockmark the slopes and, far from being unsightly, evoke feelings of admiration for the tough workmen of old who, with steel bar and gunpowder, testified to the fact that not only faith moves mountains.

On the tously ridge of Lingmell—a ridge lying south of Great Langdale—are to be found heather moorland, peaty pools, bracken, mini-groves of juniper, quarries without number and, on the lower slopes, a glorious mix of trees.

What was once a mix of indigenous species which was clear-felled every seven years or so for charcoal-burning is now an area of fewer mature trees. It is many years since coppicing the woods sustained half a dozen local crafts. (The charcoal was needed for gunpowder production at Elterwater).

At Banks Quarry I was reminded of Frank Birkett's expedition to try to re-locate a cave used by Lanty Slee. He had last visited it sixty years before. Frank had led me across heaps of slate and beside the remains of small buildings.

The way continued across mossy ground. We ducked under the branches of gnarled and ancient trees. A buzzard circled and mewed. There was a merry run of notes from a chaffinch perched on a juniper, a tree that Frank knew under its local name of "savin".

We came across the "cow fence", which proved to be a low drystone wall, said to have been made by the farmer at Baysbrown to discourage his sheep from wandering off the edge of the crags. Frank said the cave was "just a lile wee spot", with space for one man to stand up in; the cavity could not be seen from above.

Having left Frank kindling his pipe as he sat on sunbaked rocks taking in what he said, without a touch of morbidity, would be his last view of Chapel Stile and Elterwater from this place, I rounded a corner and found the natural rent in the crags, some six feet high at the front. A pile of stone lay at the mouth of the shallow cave and gave the impression of being an altar. The cleansing breeze had taken away any tang of whisky.

I returned to find Frank sitting on a sun-warmed boulder. He was pleased. "I knew it was here," he said, adding—"We've done aw reet!"

On our expedition along the airy ridge of Lingmoor, one of the last Lakeland refuges of the pine marten, Bob and I had grand views whether we looked westwards towards Coniston, eastwards into the deep trough of Great Langdale or (in due course) northwards across the alluvial plain at the very head of the dale. In clear view for most of the time were the rock turrets of the Langdale Pikes.

Lingmoor is a superb vantage point for the head of the "windy valley", as Keith Rowand, farmer at Stool End, called his part of the dale. The valley head is hard on men and stock. "It'll never change. The weather will always govern it and give us plenty of work", said Keith.

Windy valley? I asked him what was the worst wind he had experienced. He replied: "The wind that knocked down about 40 yards of wall". He switched the topic to visitors' dogs and hoped that people would keep them on leads. "It would be very nice if, when fell-walkers see worn-out shepherds and dogs coming down behind a flock of sheep, they'd stand to one side and let the old sheep go on their rightful way home".

One of the Lake Poets wrote, with tongue in cheek: "Not one day in the Lake District week can be properly called Sun-day". For a period of some weeks in winter, the sun does not shine directly on Stool End farmhouse.

Keith resigns himself to losing direct sight of the sun at his dalehead farmhouse from November 10 until the end of January. One year "the first flash of sunlight came on January 28. At about 10-30. I remember looking at my watch. I was just knocking about in the yard when the sun shone for a moment".

We completed our circuit by following the path on the lower slopes of Lingmoor, this hulk of ground blocking out most of the western sky.

It began to rain. A high precipitation does give the beck its voice and the lakes their splendour. It sustains the growth of various ferns, nourishes the grass, sends the least dedicated holidaymakers dashing for cover and is ignored by fell-walkers.

Rain gives us a perennial topic of conversation. I asked a farmer what the weather was likely to do. Even as I inquired, I thought he might reply: "I haven't seen telly forecast today".

He looked up the dale through his pale blue eyes. He stared at Lingmoor. He fixed his gaze on his booted feet. He turned to behold the surging beck and he said, weighing each word carefully: "It'll happen please itself".

The Secret Places

WAINWRIGHT did not see anything beautiful in places of industrial dereliction, such as quarries and mines, but he did visit them and was moved at the thought of centuries of bustle and noise.

He told me that silence is always more profound in places which once were noisy.

Not for him the crowds, but "the secret places that must be searched for". So, using a 6″ map, he located the old drove roads and the trails followed by packhorses.

He went into remote gills to find the traces of adits and levels where mining took place.

Illgill Head:
Above the Screes

IN NEXT to no time, Bob and I were under tree cover. Eskdale Green has a well-wooded appearance but now we were blinkered by trees. The deciduous growth was tolerable. The coniferous forest was dark, dreary, with massed trunks giving the impression of being in a repository for telegraph poles.

We crossed the River Mite, which has its nursery on the moors towards Burnmoor Tarn. The Ordnance map showed a huge expanse of green representing Miterdale Forest. Why do they make a point of naming forests which all seem to look alike?

The track from Eskdale Green to Nether Wasdale surmounted an easy slope on to Irton Fell, where Bob commanded that there should be a right turn. He promised an entry into the gee-whiz country, but first we must negotiate the cleft of Greathall Gill.

The clarty terrain between Whin Rigg and Illgill Head would be utterly dreary but for the views to the west, given good weather. The path scarcely varied in elevation and my boots collected lumps of peat.

What distinguishes this route is that view to the west. To most people, seeing it from the shores of Wastwater, Illgill Head is "Wastwater Screes", the showy western flank of a great hump of high ground.

Our little group veered from the path to the edge of the scars, from which to admire the crags and stone-strewn slopes. The famous view of Wastwater Screes is from west of the water. Then, lofty and fan-shaped, the Screes seem to leap from the water and are worthy of a place in the Norwegian fjordland.

This boulder slope of rocks which move imperceptibly at the dictates of the freeze-thaw routine and our old friend gravity, continues

97

under the water, of course, and thus has a vertical height of nearly 2,000 ft.

The Victorian climbers who gathered at Wasdale Head and humbled many a crag were not very fond of The Screes, and O G Jones is said to have called them "deadly". Walkers tempted on to the path twixt water and scree-slope have been known to use much stronger words.

Mrs Linton, the romantic, looked at the Screes with an artist's eye; they were "wonderfully soft and velvet-like" in the evening light of a summer day. Their tints were "purple, with patches of golden-brown moss set in rims of golden-green".

Wastwater itself, so often gunmetal grey or in sunshine having the blueness of sterility, was to Mrs Linton a blue-plus. She wrote of it being "blue and green and grey and purple and silver and gold by turns, with great slabs of turquoise and malachite beneath". I shuddered at the thought of mixing that lot in water-colours.

From a promontory at the head of The Screes I looked down, down, down to a stretch of water which reflected the summer sky—a uniform mid-grey tone.

Beyond Illgill Head, our interest switched to Wasdale Head. We followed a wallside until, at the 900 ft contour, Bob set course for Burnmoor and its large tarn. Now there was the familiar squelch of feet in bogland until our boots had entered firmer ground in the form of the old corpse road extending from Wasdale Head to Boot.

We quit this route for what Wainwright called "shy little Miterdale", having a butty-stop in a little amphitheatre where the river was as clear and cool as that used by Kingsley's water-babies. Now we followed the Mite's banks as best we could to reach Miterdale Head, where our feet clonked on a metalled road at Low Place Farm.

The road led us, without fuss, and in semi-wooded setting, back to the starting point at Eskdale Green.

Great Gable:
A Place for Remembrance

GIVE a child some paper, a pencil and ask him/her to draw a mountain. The result will be the outline of Great Gable from Wasdale. The pyramidal shape is etched on our minds from the earliest days of looking at picture books. It is no wonder that Gable and its attendant fells were chosen as the emblem of the Lake District National Park.

The name has a fine ring about it. Bob, consulting Wainwright at the start of our expedition from Seathwaite, chuckled for a few moments and read the master fell-walker's comment that if Great Gable were known only as Wasdale Fell, fewer people would climb it.

We climbed by Sour Milk Ghyll and Green Gable. It was that magical time of the year when daffodils bloom in the dales and patches of snow linger on the fells. At the summit of Green Gable, I began to think of butties and tea.

Bob, a veteran of this area, had not allowed himself to get excited. It was my first ascent of Gable and he had been up the hill umpteen times. Bob muttered: "Windy Gap" and fell-walkers within hearing went pale. The Gap suddenly appeared—a 600 ft almost sheer drop to where patches of snow lay in the ancient joints of the landscape. Beyond, a rock staircase made a demanding ascent of an equivalent distance to Great Gable itself.

Up there, amid the jumble of boulders, was the war memorial of the Fell and Rock Climbing Club. It was H P Cain who put forward the idea of buying a mountain and some tract of wild upland as a memorial to Club members who had died.

At one time the members had the purchase of Pillar Rock in mind, but this could not be arranged. Instead, and with much goodwill on the part of the owner, a large tract of high fells, including Great Gable, was bought for only £400, a sum that was raised without difficulty.

At the annual dinner in 1923, the deeds of the gifted land were handed over to F D Acland, representing the National Trust. The bronze plaque listing those who had died was set on a stone base as a war memorial. It was unveiled on Whit Sunday, 1924, by Dr A W Wakefield in the presence of no less than 500 people.

Between the wars, a small group of people gathered on Great Gable at the 11th hour of the 11th day of the 11th month to remember the victims of the war. It was a commemoration in which both Lionel Glaister and Ralph Mayson were especially interested, having served in the Forces during the war.

They contrived to climb the mountain with a laurel wreath that grew smaller as the years went by—not surprising, considering the large amount of photographic gear they felt they needed to record the Remembrance gathering.

Today, hundreds gather on Gable each Remembrance Sunday. Bob recalled when a breeze sprang up and a shimmering mass of artificial poppy petals drifted away through the thin mountain air. Another time, the last post was sounded by a bugler at a much lower elevation—a haunting sound, carrying far in the still air.

At the Westmorland Cairn I recalled chatting with "Rusty" Westmorland, one of the same family, at his home in Troutbeck. He was then an old man but bright-eyed and with a mind full of mountain memories.

We Wainwrighters used the Gable Traverse to reach two notable features of this challenging fell—the Sphinx Rock, which always looks to me like an Indian brave, with jutting jaw and tuft of feathers on his head, and the celebrated Napes Needle, recalling a story by Graham Sutton entitled "The Man who Broke the Needle".

We scrambled up the rocks until we overtook a climber with helmet and ropes. The idea was to photograph the Sphinx Rock with Wastdale beyond. Mist had blunted the lines of the landscape.

Napes Needle was bedecked with climbers' ropes. In 1957, *Cumbria* magazine used an article by O S MacDonell about this famous pinnacle. He mentioned his belief that the first woman to climb the Needle was a Miss Corder (accompanied by a dales yeoman farmer in 1885).

Six years later a man and woman, believed to be brother and sister, though they did not belong to the climbing fraternity, were photographed at the very top, and the picture—the usual view of the Needle—withstood scrutiny; it had not been faked.

A rope was shown dangling from the summit on the almost vertical and quite unclimbable face to the saddle that connects this isolated rock to the main crag. The photograph was carefully examined. It was seen that a number of loops had been knotted at close intervals along the whole length of the rope.

The picture also showed an elderly man standing on the saddle. He was recognised as a certain Oxford professor. Later, he told how the "climb" had been done. The climbers and some friends had carried several coils of rope and a long length of light but strong cord. Loops were knotted in one of the ropes.

A member of the party, who evidently was a cricketer and could throw with strength and accuracy, tied a stone of suitable weight to the end of the cord. After several failures, he succeeded in throwing the stone with its attached cord from the saddle over the top of the Needle so that they went down on the other side.

A rope was fixed, one end to the cord and the other end to the rope with the loops. The whole arrangement was pulled until the rope with the loops reached the top of the Needle and the other rope to the base of the rock on its further side, where two men held it firmly.

The young man of the photograph then fastened one end of a third rope to himself and the other round his sister. He climbed up the rope with the loops, putting his feet into them. He made little or no use of holds in the rock. And his sister climbed in the same way.

O S MacDonell added: "They went down the same way as they had come up. Later they managed to pull away all the ropes, so no evidence was left as to how the climb had been done, except in the photograph".

I was once shown a Gable garnet, which is not especially rare or valuable. It was found lodged in rock, just behind the Needle.

We continued, along to Sty Head and back to Borrowdale. Not long afterwards, our little party was back at Sty Head, en route for Great End. The normal contours of the landscape had been changed by drifted snow.

That day, we had planned to join the host on Gable for the Remembrance gathering, I awoke with a shiver. The temperature of my bedroom had plummeted and although it was early November the fells across the valley had a silver gleam that was not just moonlight. Several inches of snow had fallen.

We motored up an M6 with ice crackling under the car tyres and also slithered a bit on the normally fast road between Penrith and Keswick. The Borrowdale road was flooded, the hilltops powdered white, yet the woods of the valley still held all the grandeur of their tinted foliage.

At Seatoller, we heard that Honister Pass was blocked with snow. A quick way to Great Gable was out of the question and "the day was far spent".

Stan suggested Great End as an alternative perch for the Remembrance service. We would see the crowd without actually being in a crowd. And—he smirked—we would be at an elevation several yards higher than they were!

And so it was. Snow and ice crunched or crackled on the way up to Sty Head Tarn, which looked black in contrast with its pure-white setting. The few gulls flew around calling mournfully for sandwiches.

The other lads wore crampons. They walked with the briskness of automata. I half expected them to have monosyllabic voices, like Daleks. My voice, when heard occasionally, rose to a shout as I slithered and fell. Three times, an elbow was the first to touch the ground, giving me an abiding memory of the slippery path by Seathwaite Tarn and the ice-slope beyond.

We climbed in sunshine, with just a few cumulous clouds above and unending whiteness all around, except when we glimpsed the green of the coastal plain and Sellafield, surmounted by a cloud of vapour.

At the top, Great Gable came into view. We were astonished at the number of black specks representing people who had managed to get to the summit in time for the service. As the eleventh hour was indicated by my watch, we stood on Great End, silently contemplating the district's white mantle and, at our feet, the delicate ice patterns on the vegetation.

Bob was silent for a moment. He told us later he was recalling a magical morning when he traversed a fell listening to a delicate jingling sound. The sun was climbing high. The lightest of breezes swept an icy felltop and the jingling was the sound of a trillion tiny pieces of ice which had formed on the tall grasses.

They were now being blown against each other by the breeze.

Langdale Pikes:
Dungeon and Scree-slope

WE AVOID the rock turrets of the Pikes in summer, of course, for then the area is over-run by trippers.

An early tourist, Thomas West, having crossed the "Stake of Borrowdale" in the 1770s, arrived within sight of "Langdale-pike, called Pike-a-stickle, and Steel-pike". What to us are shapely fells were, to the Lakeland traveller in the days before the Romantic Age got into its swing, "awesome" and "dreadful" heights.

Mr West went further: "Here nature seems to have discharged all her useless load of matter and rock, when form was first impressed on chaos".

Normally, we have gone Pike-bagging in the off-season—the period between leaf-casting and the appearance of fresh new growth on thorn and rowan or, for the benefit of bird-watchers, between the appearance of the fieldfares, bird refugees from Scandinavia, and the hatch of raven eggs in twiggy nests on the crags.

We all enjoy watching an air display put on by a raven, which has as much character as one of the old updale Lakeland farmers. At our approach, the bird launches itself from a crag and, without beating its wings, lets the wind assist it. The raven croaks, then flicks over on to its back and flies upside down for a short spell as though revelling in the sheer joy of living.

A hoarse call, pruk, pruk, indicates its position when it has risen above a few tatters of cloud and is momentarily out of sight.

When Frank Birkett was nobbut a lad in "Gurt Langdale", a pair of ravens nesting on Pike o' Bliscoe attracted the attention of egg collectors because the female laid eggs which had some red spots on them. She was nicknamed Red Raven. The nest was always in "an awkward place" but this did not deter a keen collector, who shinned down a rope.

One man had to be rescued. He reached the ledge, popped the raven eggs in his pocket but as he climbed back his shoulders were trapped against an overhang and he had to be rescued by Frank and a friend. Such egg-collecting is now illegal, thank goodness. In the old days a clutch of raven eggs was worth £1—a sum which was then a week's wage for a farm man.

We enjoyed chatting with local farmers, one of whom called the Pikes "rough and bony". The fell-going sheep are "heafed"; they drink in a love of the native fellside with their mother's milk and tend to remain in those areas where they were reared as lambs.

The sheep of Millbeck Farm, near Dungeon Ghyll, range the adjacent fell. They meet stocks from the Borrowdale farms at High Raise and those of the Grasmere farms about Caudale Tarn.

Sometimes, we shared a sandwich or two with the sheep, mindful that it was not the right thing to do. To the sheep, a sandwich would make a pleasant change from the herby food of the fellsides and the heather that wears away its teeth in next to no time so that "twinters" [three-year-olds] have to be drafted to low country where the diet is softer.

There is no ling on those parts of the Pikes where the Greggs of Millbeck run their sheep. They dine on coarse grasses, with blaeberry as "sweet".

One of our Langdale expeditions began with the familiar 2,000 ft climb from the green floor of Great Langdale to the high crags, passing Stickle Tarn, where the water level was raised by a dam installed by the old gunpowder factory at Elterwater (which closed in 1930).

A man was employed to attend to the sluice. He went up to Stickle Tarn on Friday evening to close the sluice gates and returned on Sunday evening to open them, thus regulating water in the beck. The gunpowder company released trout into the tarn and the fish were usually poached by men using night-lines.

I began this note about the Pikes by mentioning our aversion to going there in summer. An exception was a Wainwright-inspired trip which began with a Wainwright path through Dungeon Ghyll. Deep and dark, with tumbling water, the Ghyll is a place to visit using the utmost care and, ideally, when wearing a metal helmet.

William Wordsworth knew the early stages, as far as the first big waterfall. He wrote in his Guide: "Under the Precipice adjoining the Pikes lies invisibly Stickle Tarn, and thence descends a conspicuous Torrent down the breast of the Mountain. Near the Torrent is Dungeon Gill Force, which cannot be found without a guide, who may be taken up at one of the Cottages at the foot of the Mountain".

I had known about Dungeon Ghyll, of course, but had not previously explored it. The usual way of climbing the Pikes—and one heartily recommended in favour of the stygian horrors of the gill—is the popular tourist path: the one by Stickle Ghyll. That path stays on the surface and has been wonderously reinforced by large stones set side by side to avert the decline of a popular route into a muddy way half as wide as the fell.

Dungeon Ghyll, the deep, water-carved gash in the fair face of Great Langdale, is not for your average tourist. It is for the hale, hearty—and daft, involving over 2,100 feet of ascent. Mr Wainwright has indicated a route in his pictorial guide to the area; anyone who deviates should first know a lot about rock-climbing to be safe.

As we booted up in the car park near the New Dungeon Ghyll, I felt a slight irritation at the Victorian partiality for spelling the name "ghyll" rather than the straight-forward "gill". What was good enough for the Norsemen and for W G Collingwood, that perceptive writer about Lakeland scenery and traditions, is most certainly good enough for us.

Wainwright considered that Gill is the proper name. "Ghyll is a poetical affectation: it is too well established at Dungeon Ghyll to be altered now..." We followed his Route 2, "an adventurous route, unfrequented and pathless in the ravines, and involving some easy but steep scrambling in impressive surroundings".

We negotiated a well-sprung, anti-herdwick sheep gate, then turned left and moved up to a stile, coming under the unblinking stare of sheep which had settled down after breakfast to engage in that boring but necessary task of cud-chewing.

The sheep gave way grudgingly. They were on the fellside by the right of 1,000 generations. We were there for a couple of hours at the most.

We entered the gill proper with a feeling of elation, not dread, having arrived at the time when the sunlight illuminated it like some gigantic spotlight, stripping the gorge of its shadows—and terror.

A grey wagtail flew off. A common wren sang at a volume much louder than would seem possible for a tiny bird. The wren was using Dungeon Gill as an echo-chamber.

The Victorians loved waterfalls. As Norman Nicholson wrote: "Waterfalls were so obviously ornamental, so tasteful, so discreet and damp and crepuscular—the kind of small-scale fanciful landscape they would have constructed for themselves had they been God".

Norman, afflicted by a lung complaint, had to observe Lakeland from the roadside. He must have envied those he saw taking to the heights—or "plunging" into the likes of Dungeon Ghyll.

Wainwright's magnificent little map indicates a series of obstacles, the first of which—well beyond the Force—is a 40 ft cascade "avoided by a steep slope on the left". The water does not tumble or roar but slides, white like spilt milk, into a pool of clear water.

The second obstacle is a choke of boulders. Wainwright mentions that the visitor passes through this area by trial and error; a way might then be found free of difficulty. We opted for the beckside route, avoiding boulders that looked half the size of bungalows.

We did not regret the choice. In one of its most attractive reaches, the water was spanned by a natural rock bridge formed of two boulders lodged end to end. I stopped to listen to another ringing aria from a wren.

We scrambled from the damp, dark ravine, leaving the upper part to the experts. Ahead lay the seamed grey form of Harrison Stickle.

Another unusual approach to the Pikes is via Stickle Tarn, Jack's Rake and Pavey Ark. The Rake is a diagonal route across the face of the crag. It is classifiable as an "easy" rock climb or a difficult scramble.

Jack's Rake is usually shunned by ordinary fell-walkers in winter but they happily queue to ascend on good days in high summer, when the rake admits one person a minute and there is an impression, from seeing their distant, colourful forms against the dark rock, of a string of beads dangling from Pavey Ark.

The approach is through an area of ankle-cracking scree and boulders. On the ascent, I kept most of my attention on the holds, but was also aware that the damp and mossy areas held butterwort in delicate flower.

The path turned, broke from cover so that there was rock on one side, a grassy slope on the other. In due course I reached the Great Gully and was looking for Wainwright's prominent pinnacle, marking the end of the climb.

I dutifully visited the summits of the Pikes and then I realised an old ambition, descending the upper part of a 2,000 ft scree slope to visit the district's first-known industrial enterprise—the mass production of stone axe-heads and associated implements.

We negotiated what looked like a most unstable slope high on Pike o' Stickle, the second of the Langdale Pikes. Stan said it was not so much a factory as an artificial cave. And that it was "just out of sight".

I believed him and took a clattering, slithering course over pieces of volcanic tuff. The angle was a little too steep for comfort, but one cannot expect too much comfort where the ground falls away for 2,000 ft in half a mile.

Which route did the commuting Stone Age workmen take to reach this factory site, which was used over 4,000 years ago? There would be some paths on the sides of the Pikes, and Neolithic muscles were doubtless accustomed to negotiating them.

The life of Neolithic man was short and none too merry, usually ending with the joints locked up with arthritis, but for men in their prime the hill would present few difficulties beyond the possibility of meeting some of the more aggressive members of a rich and varied fauna.

In those days, the Lakeland wildwood was tenanted by wolves, bears and wild swine. The wild boar was fierce enough but there was nothing to match the ferocity of a female defending her piglets, which were striped like humbugs.

I kept Stan's figure well in view during the descent to the ancient axe-making site, even though I stood periodically to give my leg muscles time to stop vibrating. The scree was alive. There was never a moment of complete silence as frost-weakened stones were coaxed into movement by the heat of the summer sun.

Did the knappers of axe-heads on Pike o' Stickle take the scree slide at the start of the homeward journey? Or did they stay on the heights for days on end? They must have been commuters, for man cannot live by axe-heads alone.

It was surely a summer industry. Did they chat to each other, these pioneer factory operatives on the scree at Pike o' Stickle? What did they talk about? Assuredly, there would be a grunt now and again as a piece of rock being worked was spoiled by careless knapping—or someone trapped a finger!

At the approach of autumn, the workmen would transfer themselves to one of the sites in the low country, such as a nice sandy beach area at the coast where the products might be smoothed using quartz sand. Sandstone grinders gave the axe-head its special edge.

With such implements as The Cumbrian Axe, and with fiery torches, the men of the New Stone Age swiftly re-fashioned the upland landscape. The Great Cumbrian Axe—repeat the words slowly, with an element of drama—helped to sustain the advance of the frontier beyond the already settled areas into the wilderness.

The rock turrets of the Langdale Pikes attract hosts of tourists. Not many of them risk life and limb by going off down the scree, taking the low road to the dale. Astonishingly, the site of the axe factory lay forgotten for many centuries. A place that had been famous in prehistoric Britain was gradually closed down, its workers being made redundant by the arrival of iron axes.

Then, in the 1940s, a visitor who was climbing in the area just happened to notice that some of the fine-grained, greenish-grey tuff from the Borrowdale Volcanic Series had been tampered with and that, scattered around, were unfinished axe-heads. In the following years, the site was picked over by visitors to such good effect that the National Trust, who own that area, would be delighted if some were returned.

Cumbrian axes have been found in all parts of Britain. It has been theorised that bartering for such objects may have taken place in the circles and henges where families assembled periodically for religious ceremonies and other social activities. Was there a Cumbrian Axe Bargain Stall at Castlerigg near Keswick?

Stan found some good pieces of shattered rock but he did not remove them, concluding that the work was University Geology Party, c1989.

I returned to valley level by a major path, not the scree slope. Wainwright mentioned that "expert scree-runners will come down the open gully . . . and reach the valley-bottom in Mickleden in a matter of minutes, but ordinary mortals will find this route very trying to the temper, though it is probably the safest way in mist and the most sheltered in bad weather".

Looking back at the scree slope and reflecting on the factory in the mist, I pondered on the changes that have taken place in the business of toppling a tree. Those working in the Lakeland forests today use—band saws!

Another day at the head of Great Langdale we left a car at the big park near New Dungeon Ghyll and strode across the valley to join the footpath leading to Pike o' Blisco, a path which, within our remembrance, had been little more than a faint mark on the landscape. It was now an unsightly mush of peaty ground bearing the deep imprints of modern boots.

These had stripped away the vegetation, creating a channel in which rainwater could gather with a scouring effect. With the grass and peat gone, an assortment of stones was exposed. Walkers who found it awkward to follow the line of stones added to the width of the path by traversing the edge, breaking through more vegetation and turning the thin layer of ground into a porridge-like mass that would be swept away to the dale by the next violent storm.

We climbed Pike o' Blisco, went on to Cold Pike (less visited and as yet not grossly eroded by boots) and then headed for the mist and Crinkle Crags, where we had no difficulty in finding the path, even over rock. Many visitors had slurred or pounded their way across the "crinkles".

We descended The Band, returning to Langdale, concerned about the disfigurement of the fells and glad that paths were being given a durable and inconspicuous surface using native stones in a time-honoured way.

Building The Mountains

WHEN the millionth Wainwright book had been sold, I wrote an article for *Cumbria* magazine. It was hastily (too hastily) typed and posted to AW, who returned it promptly, smothered with green ink where he had made corrections.

I felt that his testy little letter mentioning the multitude of typing and grammatical errors was justified.

I had mentioned the time when he started to draw pictures of the Lakeland fells. He discovered the joy of mountain-building on a blank sheet of paper. "Let's do Great Gable," he might say. And he would promptly draw the fell in ink, with a steel-nibbed pen.

He told me that the sketches were based on photographs. The camera he used had been acquired second-hand. It had "various contrivances". All that mattered to AW was how to replace a film and "which knob to press to take a picture".

His aim, he added, was to draw mountains, "not in a romantic and imaginative sense, but as they are".

WRM.

Back o' Skiddaw:
Nowt But Scenery

IN THE clarty country "back o' Skidda", where clay and peat are thatched with bracken and heather, the river Caldew has its beginnings within sight of Skiddaw House, which is said to have been the loneliest dwelling in Lakeland.

If it hadn't been for Skiddaw House, a former lodging place of shepherds, the vast space between Skiddaw and the rim of the northern fells would have nowt but scenery, to quote a visitor from industrialised Lancashire.

Having left one car just beyond the former sanatorium on the edge of Blencathra, we travelled in the other through Mungrisedale (named after Mungo, a name for St Kentigern) and parked the second car in Mosedale.

I once asked a Mungrisedale man about the source of the river Caldew and I was directed to Mosedale. "Turn left where you see a telephone kiosk," he said, using a variant of the common directions in which reliance is placed on the names of pubs.

In Mosedale, I found that the river Caldew was already a noisy, brawling torrent. Both Caldew and Cald-beck, which joins it near the village of that name, could be derived from keld, meaning spring. Having had an infusion of cold mountain water, the Caldew surges down a wooded valley and in due course the water seethes as it descends the bays [weirs] of Dalton on its way to join the Eden at Carlisle.

The secluded valley of Mosedale, nursery of the river Caldew, has a Scottishness about it in the ruggedness of its hills, a river with a delicate shade of brown, like whisky, and enough heather and bracken to give the area a rich orange-brownness through the colder end of the year.

We left the car not far from the Round House, some six miles from Caldew's source. The house is not round; it has twelve sides. Who cared about a name on a healthful day when we had sunshine and a warm breeze on our faces; when we heard little else but the river and drawling curlews.

The owner of the Round House told me that the Caldew had been known to rise and fall two feet in a day. This is a musical river on a calm summer day when the water level is low. Then people sitting in the water to cool off may hear the clinking of stone against stone on the bed of the river.

We strode along the track to the old Carrock Mine, once a prime source of tungsten but closed now. Tungsten has a rather special use in making steel for armaments and the Carrock mine has tended to thrive and flop as periods of war have been followed by years of peace.

Carrock Fell is a highly mineralised, boulder-littered hill at the edge of rocky Lakeland. Beyond where the landscape had been sterilised by mining, the path lay between rocks and gorse. We none the less watched our feet in case we tripped over a kneeling or even crawling geologist.

As the gradient lessened, we experienced the usual "false summit" and then stood on the true one with its defensive wall. Carrock was an ideal place for a hill fort.

Everywhere was evidence of mining. This area was one thought to be "worth all England else", a reference to the mineral deposits.

Charles Dickens sent his Two Idle Apprentices up Carrock Fell in 1857. At first the ascent was delusively easy, the sides of the mountain sloping gradually and composed of soft spongy turf, very tender and pleasant to walk upon.

"After a hundred yards or so, however, the verdant scene and the easy slope disappeared, and the rocks began. Not noble, massive rocks, standing upright, keeping a certain regularity in their positions, and possessing, now and then, flat tops to sit upon, but little irritating, comfortless rocks, littered about anyhow by Nature... bruisers of tender toes and trippers-up of wavering feet".

The route lay north east, skirting the head of Drygill to reach High Pike (2,157 ft) with yet more remains—this time of a shepherd's cottage, with a slate seat on which to sit while munching sandwiches and also taking in the vista of Scottish as well as Pennine hills.

This rolling, grassy landscape must be sheep-sick after many centuries of grazing. On my first visit, years ago, I chatted with Harrison and John Wilson and heard about shepherds' meets and the local shepherds' feast.

On the last Monday in July, shepherds met on t'fell at Wylie Ghyll. A barrel of beer had been taken up on the back of a horse. The barrel was "tapped" and then allowed to settle down overnight. "They couldn't have done that now; t'wad have gone!" The place chosen for the meet seemed remote until it was realised that this event was being attended by men from a wide area.

On the first Monday after the 29th of October, the shepherds met at Black Hazel, just opposite the Ghyll. It was colder then, and the men took with them something stronger than ale—whisky or rum.

The shepherds' feast was summat special, taking place on the first Monday in December at five places in rotation—at Mungrisedale, Threlkeld, Bassenthwaite, Uldale and Caldbeck. The centrepiece of this feast was a large tatie pot into which mutton, black puddings and potatoes had been dropped. "It was near Christmas, so they always had some plum pudding; it was a real good do".

We walked easily in this rolling, grassy landscape, following our early conquests with Great Lingy Hill and organising a butty-stop at its its wooden hut formerly used by shooters and now providing shelter for anyone who wishes to use it.

A muddy crossing of Grainsgill Beck is necessary en route to Knott (2,329 ft) the centrepiece of the Uldale Fells. Thence to Little and Great Sca Fells.

The dome of Great Calva (2,265 ft) is an excellent vantage point. We looked through the V-shaped notch between Skiddaw and Blencathra and then over the green and brown, treeless wilderness of Skiddaw Forest.

We had a steady descent to Skiddaw House, with the infant Caldew in view. Here we were in the so-called Skiddaw Forest, but with only a few gale-blasted pines behind the House to lend credibility to what we now think of as a thickly wooded area. (In fact, the name forest comes from "foris", which in Norman times was land set apart for hunting purposes).

Here, at the very head of the Caldew Valley, was the building which is said to be the loneliest in Lakeland, if not in the country. It stands on an eastern slope of Skiddaw (3,054 ft) at an elevation of 1,550 ft and is not one house but a whole row of cottages, where shepherds and their families could stay for weeks at a time.

For many years, from the death of a shepherd called Pearson Dalton, whose regular home was Fell Side near Caldbeck, Skiddaw House was ruined though from 1973 part of the property was maintained by the Border Bothies Association.

Behind the house is a conifered tract where the trees seem about ready to give up their uneven fight with nature in the form of high winds and stinging frost.

A track that was kind to our aching feet conveyed us through the notch to Troutbeck.

The Old Man of Coniston

ARTHUR Ransome, author of the classic children's stories with Lakeland settings, transformed The Old Man of Coniston into Kanchenjunga.

To Wainwright, it was the Matterhorn, with the village of Coniston as the Lakeland equivalent of Zermatt.

Our little party, while mopping up some of the "Wainwrights" on the Coniston Fells, regarded t'Old Man that day as an exercise in quickly gaining our operational height, in this case 2,631 ft. It ensured that the rest of the day's walking would be relatively easy.

We had first viewed Coniston Old Man and his retainers from near Brantwood. John Ruskin, whose home this was, became a specialist in Lakeland views, such as the one of Lunesdale from near the church at Kirkby Lonsdale and the prospect of fells and water from Friar's Crag near Keswick.

One Old Man (Ruskin) gloried in his vantage point for another Old Man, which has such a southerly location he could refer to the Coniston group as "the first great upthrust of Mountain Britain".

Ruskin was maffly [mentally confused] in his old age and his relatives kept him a virtual prisoner at Brantwood. Sometimes he slipped away to visit Coniston. He usually found his way to the home of a woman, now married, who had once worked for him. She fussed over him, fed him and listened to him until a posse from Brantwood collected him.

How do I know all this? It was among the recollections of a small boy, a nephew of the lady of the story, who witnessed it. He was 106 years of age when I chatted with him.

Another tale about Coniston came from Norman Nicholson, the Lakeland poet who lived at Millom. We were chatting beside the fire at his home (which had also been his birthplace) when he recalled the family shop and some of the customers, one of them living in

Coniston. Father introduced Young Norman to him. And Norman eventually asked: "Are you Coniston Old Man?"

Our visit to Coniston began with the clink of tea cups against saucers in a local cafe. We did not dawdle, being anxious to keep ahead of the crowd of fell-walkers and school parties who were aiming to reach the summit cairn.

The weather looked "settled". The Old Man is not especially hospitable and there has been no proper shelter as such since early last century, when the Ordnance surveyors who were busy filling in blanks on the map found on the summit of the fell a simple stone structure which was used in bad weather by shepherds and a few intrepid tourists.

Insensitively, the surveyors paid a local labourer £5 to demolish it. He did not complain, earning one pound an hour while the job lasted. There were stone pillars, of course, three in particular, their names being Old Man, his Wife and Son.

As we began the ascent from Coniston, I re-told Wilf Nicholson's story about the Scout group who visited a fell farm and requested a camping site. The Scouts were directed to a small croft. The leader returned to the farmhouse, saying that the land sloped too much for the pitching of tents. The farmer explained that "God gave us so mich land we hed to pile it in gurt big heaps".

On to the big heaps the quarrymen and miners added lesser heaps of dross, for The Old Man has yielded slate for building and copper ore to be smelted at "bloomeries" in the woods by the lake. The copper was then transported by boat to Nibthwaite and from here went by road to Ulverston or Greenodd.

In days of yore (pre-1974, when the Boundary Commission messed about with the boundaries) Coniston was in that southern wedge-shaped slice of the Lakeland "cake" which belonged to Lancashire. This would give added pleasure to Lancashire-born Wainwright, even though by implication Lancashire brains and brass had industrialised the area. As AW was fond of saying, there is no beauty in dereliction.

Industry took precedence over farming, though eventually industry had its day. I recall chatting with a former vicar of Coniston in his study when the subject of his "flock" was broached. He said: "In this part of the world there are white sheep on the fell and black sheep

116

in the valley".

He, poor soul, was a southerner who had arrived in the region with romantic ideas about Wordsworth and daffodils. Not only were the dale farmers surprisingly ignorant about Wordsworth, but daffodils did not appeal to them either, unless someone could bring out a variety that grew wool.

Arthur Ransome, a Leeds lad who spent boyhood holidays at Nibthwaite, near the outflow of Coniston Water, was carried up Coniston Old Man as a baby in the arms of his father; eventually, as a lively lad, he got to know the lake, its islets and the Old Man.

The fictitious expedition to Kanchenjunga (based soundly on factual incidents) was from the north, the direction we had chosen. Ransome's engaging characters, and especially the Swallows and Amazons, came to mind as we moved clinkingly over slate on a climb of 2,450 ft in about three miles. We followed a zig-zag route between lichened boulders and tufts of hardy grasses.

At every footfall we were conscious of walking where others had already trodden. T'Owd Man is not just the name of a fell but is also a collective name for past generations of miners, most of them forgotten as individuals. Mining activity has led to the map being speckled with odd names like Paddy End, Simon's Nick and Cobbler Holme.

Simon's Nick is named after a man who obtained large quantities of rich ore from the fissure. He was the only person who could find it and, naturally, he refused to discuss the matter with the other miners—until one evening, in the Black Bull, he became so drunk he gave full details to those around him. Simon said that he had been assisted in his quest for metal by—the fairies!

From that moment, the fairies forsook him; he became careless in his work and died when, not paying enough attention to what he was doing when placing a charge of gunpowder, he was blown into pieces when it went off prematurely.

Our good friend Mrs Linton, the Victorian novelist, was in Coppermines Valley when the mines were still active. "And in truth [she wrote] they are inhabited; and not only with human beings; for they are also swarming with rats, which get sustained by some mysterious process of assimilation unexplained, seeing that they having nothing but quartz and copper to eat; if they do not take clay for a diversion".

She saw a huge waterwheel, "turning round as if for the benefit of the crows and ravens only; but in reality it hoists the kibbles in the mines below to a certain level, and does its business none the less effectually because remotely".

Ahead of us, the path took an unrelenting course to the skyline beside scars and screes and traces of quarrying activity. It was not an unduly difficult climb.

Low Water was as blue-black as Stephen's ink, and also flat calm against a Brim Fell backdrop. Wainwright wrote that this tarn (for such it really is, despite the grander name of Water) was a good place for giving up the climb of Coniston Old Man—and going to sleep! A lullaby is provided by Low Water Beck, which blends its water with Levers Water Beck and becomes Church Beck in a relatively short journey to the lake.

Ravens haunt the Coniston Fells. The author of a book called *The Old Man or Ravings and Ramblings Round Conistone* (1849) mentioned the ravens that nested on Kernel Crag. They rarely nested in peace for the shepherds took their eggs or killed the fledglings. It was noticed that however many ravens were destroyed, there was usually a breeding pair on the Crag above Coppermines Valley.

"When one of the parents has been shot in the brooding season, the survivor has immediately been provided with another helpmate...It happened, a year or two since, that both the parent birds were shot whilst the nest was full of unfledged young, and their duties were immediately undertaken by a couple of strange ravens, who attended assiduously to the wants of the orphan brood, until they were fit to forage for themselves".

As we left the stonescape and felt short grass underfoot, our eyes quested for the cairn. And when that was in view we acquired an extra spring in our feet at the thought of butty-and-tea.

Ransome's youngsters used a rope as a climbing aid, which was much more fun than merely walking. As the summit came into sight, they "wriggled out of the loops in the rope and raced for it", as Ransome wrote in *Swallowdale*. "John and Nancy reached the cairn almost together. Roger and Titty came next. Mate Susan had stopped to coil the rope and Mate Peggy had waited to help her carry it".

Wainwright drew the summit of Coniston Old Man with the title

"Typical summit scene". Millions of people have seen his simple sketch showing, on the left, a clutch of tourists looking for Blackpool Tower. Standing beside the summit are four Boy Scouts, while to the right is the "solitary fellwalker, bless him, looking north to the hills".

When thirty-three and one-third percent of our butties had been consumed—we are methodical in our catering—we walked along the ridge to Swirl How and commenced our blundering about the Coniston Fells, enjoying the wide views of land and sea. We saw the gleam of sunlight on the estuaries of Duddon, Leven and Kent. Bob said that if the weather had been sharp, we would have viewed the Isle of Man.

On Coniston Water, a plume of white smoke rose from the funnel of the restored Furness Railway steamboat *Gondola,* now owned by the National Trust.

For us, there was the elation of high ridge walking before returning via the Walna Scar road to the flesh-pots of Coniston, the Zermatt of Lakeland.

Paper By The Ton

WAINWRIGHT was busy with his seven Pictorial Guides over a spell of 13 years, from 1952 until 1965, "both years inclusive as the buff forms say".

When, in July, 1953, he had prepared a hundred pages of pictures and prose, he scrapped them and re-did the work so that he might justify (even up) the line ends. Complete justification was not always possible, but he was pleased with the tidier appearance of his work.

The millionth guide book was sold in 1986. It was a staggering thought that, during my visits to the *Westmorland Gazette,* I had watched the first sheets being printed from metal blocks, and that up to the production of the millionth copy, no less than 200 tons of paper had been used.

Blencathra:
Climbing into the Saddle

IT WAS done on impulse. We had intended to climb in the west, but Blencathra was pin-sharp and clear of mist: like a multi-toned cut-out propped against a sky of ultramarine blue. Yanking on the wheel of the car, I left the main road to Keswick and drove through Threlkeld, leaving the car at an official park as a change from road verges and dykesides.

The stomachs of my companions were still heading down the A66 when I cheerfully explained: "I've never bagged Blencathra". They did no object.

Having passed Blencathra hundreds of times and chatted about it at length with "Rusty" Westmorland, one of our greatest climbers, whose old age was being spent at Troutbeck, I was frustrated at not humbling The Peak of Devils, which is one explanation of the name.

The earliest known form is "Rackes of Blenkarthure" (1589), which some people link with the ubiquitous King Arthur. Saddleback, a relatively modern name, may have been prompted by a description penned by Edward Baines in 1790, that "the whole side or back of the hill appears like a smooth, sloping saddle for some Brobdingnagian rider".

Now I was itching to climb into the saddle after my second attempt, the first having ended in disappointment. We had begun the climb using the arete known as Halls Fell on the enthusiastic recommendation of Wainwright. This, he said, is "positively the finest way to any mountain top in the district". Not everyone agrees. Some consider it too short for that distinction.

The arete scores a bulls-eye, taking the walker directly to the summit. We were defeated by the wind—a "lazy" wind which, instead of taking the trouble to go round us, did its best to go through. More to the point, it threatened to make us airborne.

So we descended and contoured to Souther Fell where, in the absence of the famous spectral army, seen in the 1730s, we photographed each other as we leaned against the wind.

On my second attempt, in settled weather, Blencathra was ours. We could see every detail of what an old friend Tom Bowker calls "a mountain wall 2,500 feet high and almost three miles long, buttressed by flying ridges and cleft with deep shadowy hollows".

We huffed and we puffed and we clambered on to the top, ritualistically placing a small stone on top of the cairn before traversing the escarpment to Blease Fell Top and returning by way of the "saddle", where we found the white cross, formed of pieces of quartz by one energetic visitor, Harold Robinson of Threlkeld.

Then—in my case, emotionally spent—we used the slopes of Foule Crag to drop to a col, where a simple stroll led to the summit of Bannerdale Crags, which forms a mile long escarpment. We walked the ridge to Bowscale Fell, and having descended to its tarn we thought of the legend of the two immortal trout as recorded soppily by Wordsworth:

> Both the undying fish that swim
> In Bowscale Tarn did wait on him;
> The pair were servants of his eye
> In their immortality...

Bob sat on a rock and read the appropriate pieces from Wainwright. On this occasion, AW's prose outshone the Wordsworthian verse.

Fleetwith Pike:
The Hollow Mountain

I SAW my first mountain-ringlet butterfly on Fleetwith Pike. Small and dark, the butterfly seemed far too delicate for life on a wind-blasted fell at over 2,000 ft above sea level. Yet here was a descendant of those ringlet butterflies that became established on the high grasslands of Lakeland as conditions became warmer following what is now popularly known as the Ice Age.

Fleetwith Pike is a huge tract of high ground lying between the head of Buttermere and Honister Hause. The pike itself, which I take to be the summit, displays itself best from near Gatesgarth, where it is shapely. I recall a summer morning watching the Nelsons hand-clipping their herdwick sheep at Gatesgarth Farm. Now and again I could not resist glancing at the the lofty western spur of Fleetwith basking in the sun under a sky of ultramarine blue.

Equally well known to visitors is the other end of Fleetwith Pike. I refer to the monstrous wall of tormented rock and fan-like screes known as Honister Crag which casts a deep shadow over a road which veers this way and then when avoiding the worst parts of a boulder-field and is beloved by advertisers who want to photograph a new car in an awesome setting.

Hugh Walpole, who wrote the Herries novels about an old-time family in the Lakeland dales country, let them spend far more time in Borrowdale than Buttermere though in the book entitled *Rogue Herries*, Francis is taken by a thin-faced vagabond to meet a gipsy girl living in a cave at the back of Honister Crag.

Walpole wrote: "On the brow of the hill the man took Herries' arm, led him over boulders, dipped down the shelving turf, then pushed up again on the hinder shoulder of Honister...He could see icily blue, the thin end of Buttermere Lake far below".

When the mountain-ringlet butterfly fluttered into our lives, we were on a walking circuit which began at Gatesgarth car park and included Wainwright's favourite little fell, Haystacks, where we toured its knolls and tarnlets.

No ridge links Haystacks with Fleetwith. We crossed open moor and beside some of the disused slate quarries. We did so pursued by a Walpole-style rainstorm: "It was as though a spirit with inky hair strode the fell and passed, blowing a great horn summoning his army! They could see the rain sweeping from the farthest horizon in curtains of gauze, blowing, bending, but never breaking".

Our good fell-walking friend Charlie Emett once sent us a letter in which he quoted a verse from Charles Baron Bowen:

> The rain it raineth on the just
> And also on the unjust fella;
> But chiefly on the just, because
> The unjust steals the just's umbrella.

In our case we were at the edge of a thunderstorm zone which released such savagery on the central fells, with attendant lightning, that several walkers were struck and at least two died. One of our Wainwright widows, left for the afternoon in a tent in a camping area at Keswick, found the climatic excessively trying. She uttered a long and fervent prayer for deliverance.

We were in sunshine at the cairn on Fleetwith Pike. The big storm was grumbling around the horizon. In our pleasant setting of ling and grass, we gazed out on two of the trio of lakes in the Buttermere valley and on some giants among the fells—High Crag, High Stile and Red Pike.

Later, from the edge of Honister Crag, I saw familiar features on a Liliputian scale. Toy cars ascended to Honister Hause. Tiny multi-coloured dots were parties of ramblers. Boulders I knew to be getting on for house-size looked like so many pebbles.

A visitor to Honister marvels at the energy of generations of quarrymen who honeycombed Honister Crag with galleries and constructed short railways to abstract the very best slate for sale. The quarrying days are now over but the spirit of the enterprise lingers on in the minds of men who worked here.

John Hind, of Rosthwaite, used to tell me about the slog up Honister Pass to work and about the conditions below ground. "We were at least away from any bad weather". Richard Brownrigg, the fourth generation of his family to make a living quarrying slate, told me about when "the wind is in the crack".

The wind blowing up from Buttermere was split into two currents by the fells. The turbulence was re-united violently and noisily on the face of Honister Crag. A man died when the boisterous wind picked him up and hurled him over the side of the Crag.

Mr Brownrigg's great-great-grandfather worked at the top of Yew Crag, which faces Honister Crag across the valley. The work was "blood for money" for slate dressed on the spot was then packed on a sled, which hurtled down the handiest scree slope to the road far below, with the man riding behind and controlling it as best he could. He, pour soul, then had to clamber back up the crag with the sled for another load.

Some quarrymen lived at shacks on the felltop. One day, the wind was so severe that it blew a stream back upon itself. Water was dashed against the windows of the shack, giving the impression to its occupants that rain was falling heavily. So they did not leave their lodgings that day!

It was an uncomfortable descent from Fleetwith to Gatesgarth, and we were saddened by a close view of a white cross, commemorating Fanny Mercer, who fell here and was killed in 1887.

Wainwright mentioned the absence of a path on the top of Low Raven and a "thin" path elsewhere. We were shocked by the state of the lowest stretch and felt most uneasy as we completed the descent. It was a jubilant moment when we reached ground that held no "terra" and had plenty of "firma".

Castle Crag:
Vantage Point for Borrowdale

BOB has a particular fancy for Castle Crag, which is like a giant molar in the Jaws of Borrowdale, as you can see if you behold the entrance to the valley from Friars Crag, Derwentwater. Bob mentioned Castle Crag a dozen times before the requisite expedition was planned. We would take in Castle Crag and other handy peaks.

He had been keeping Castle Crag at the back of his mind as a very special feature, even though it is only 985 ft high, which is hardly enough height for half a mountain.

Bagging Castle Crag followed a dutiful visit to Friars Crag for one of Mr Ruskin's favourite views—and a first glimpse of the big tooth in the Jaws of Borrowdale.

I took a video camera for a sequence taking in Derwentwater and the distant fells. There would be only natural sounds like bird song on the sound-track. I "shushed" the others and soon the camera was "running".

The silence (for even the birds had gone quiet) was shattered by a single loud, crunching sound. I traced it to a young man who was occupying a public seat and had just closed his teeth on a large potato crisp taken from a newly-opened packet. He kindly desisted until I had completed my video sequence.

We felt somewhat overdressed as we followed an ice cream-sucking family for a saunter from Grange through the woods of sessile oak and by the crystal-clear Derwent ("the oak river"). We chatted to a spirited old man from a northern city who, when asked about his health, said: "Nay—t'main burner's gone out, but t'pilot light's still on!"

A woman sat writing her holiday postcards, which presumably were of the wish-you-were-here theme, hoping that none of the recipients would be impelled to pack their bags and join her in the Lakes. Early tourists wrote reflectively and at length.

Borrowdale had "fantastic" rocky scenes and a "rugged" entrance. "One rock elbows out and turns the road directly against another". The sides of Borrowdale were decked with woods, "trees grow from pointed rocks and rocks appear like trees". Who nowadays would relate the rapid speed of the river Derwent to that of the Rhone?

Not far from the village, where camping takes place, we had our first good view of Castle Crag. It rose in high wooded splendour. Little effort was needed to picture a castellated building on top and to have a damsel in distress leaning from a window on a turret, waiting for her prince to arrive. Walt Disney would have been enchanted by Castle Crag.

I once tried to climb this eminence from the side nearest the river. To an experienced climber it would have presented few difficulties but I was soon frustrated by a paucity of hand-holes.

Like the moon, Castle Crag has some interesting features on its far side. We might have approached it from Rosthwaite, walking down a lane, across the Derwent and through the fields to meet the path where it is composed of fragments of rock which clink and slither underfoot.

Instead we were approaching from Grange, up the stony gap between Castle Crag and Goat Crag. There followed a steep but short path to the top.

Thomas West, author of one of the first Lakeland guide books (1778), chose Castle Crag as one of the viewpoints or stations at which tourists could indulge their love of the picturesque by simply standing and gawping.

West wrote: "From the top of Castlecrag in Borrowdale, there is a most astonishing view of the lake and vale of Keswick, spread out to the north in the most picturesque manner. . . This truly secreted spot is completely surrounded by the most horrid, romantic mountains that are in this region of wonders; and whoever omits this *coup d'oeil* hath probably seen nothing equal to it".

Castle Crag was given to the National Trust in 1920 by Sir William Hamer. It was a gift in memory of his son, Lieut John Hamer, and also the men of Borrowdale who fell in the first world war.

Stan pointed out the contrasting views. Northwards, it was like looking over a rain forest, so closesly packed were the Borrowdale oaks. Southwards, the view was of the upper dale, with a reasonable amount of woodland on the lower slopes of the fells, and trees lining the banks of the Derwent, but most of the ground consisting of verdant grassland.

The oakwoods of Borrowdale hide quarries and caves. Just across the river from Castle Crag is a monstrous boulder known as the Bowder Stone.

Castle Crag has a fringe of birch around its base and pine trees send their roots between the rocks at higher elevations. The Crag was described by Harriet Martineau of Ambleside as "a high rock, almost detached from the surrounding mountains, and said to have been used as a natural fortress, first by the Romans, then the Saxons and afterwards the Furness Monks. . . ."

She might have mentioned the generations of quarrymen who created the path that leads to Castle Crag and began the systematic destruction of the Crag itself. Quarrymen took over from nature, transforming the crag with the help of gunpowder and iron bars.

In one of the man-made caves lived an eccentric named Millican Dalton, who died as recently as 1947, aged 80. In summer, he occupied a cave by day and had an adjacent cave as his bedroom.

Dalton lived a sort of backwoodsman's life, making all his own clothes and periodically launching a raft on the Derwent. He migrated to Epping Forest for the winter.

Mrs Linton referred to "the great purple caverns" of Borrowdale which seemed close at hand, "as if you could fling a stone against the very brow of Castle Crag, blocking up the way". Wordsworth, in a prose work, referred to Castle Crag as "springing out from the midst of [the rocks and woods], crowned with the antiquated circle of a Roman emcampment", which is unlikely, though Iron Age and Dark Age use is not ruled out by authorities.

Norman Nicholson likened the shape of the hill to an inverted ice-cream cone and mentioned the delight it gave to the 18th century painters.

Thomas West summed it all up, for his own time and for the future, when he wrote: "From the summit of this rock, the views are so singularly great and pleasing that they ought never to be omitted".

Robinson:

Fools On The Moss

WE CALLED for a crack (chit-chat) at Gill Brow. A trip to Newlands
Valley would be unthinkable without visiting Ike and May Wilson. Ike
talks in a quiet but delightfully expressive Lakeland way and May,
truly Lakeland in her hospitality, provides hot tea and warm, rum-
buttered scones.

On one occasion, a time of family celebration, there was something
a bit stronger than tea and also some cake, reminding me of the story
of the Lakeland farm man who was kept on basic rations. One day he
was given a piece of cake—and he never wanted another piece of
bread as long as he lived!

Bob and Stan are old friends of the Wilsons. Bob recalls a dismally
murky and wet evening when he and his wife Pauline motored in the
Keswick area looking for overnight accommodation. By great good
fortune, they saw the sign for Gill Brow.

I had chatted with Ike's brother at Mungrisedale and realised that
here was a family steeped in Lakeland farming lore.

From the road, you have a good view of the rooftops of Gill Brow.
And from the farmyard, there is a stunning panoramic view of the
stubby vale of Newlands and its shapely guardian fells.

Bob had considered it was time to climb Robinson. He told me about
it when we reached Newlands. Or, rather, when I asked where we
were going he pointed, and his outstretched arm seemed to be lined
up with what remained visible of last night's moon.

Robinson, a somewhat bland fell, is best seen from Newlands. Second best is the view from the Hause, twixt Newlands and Buttermere. Then Robinson peeps shyly over its flanking scars.

From Newlands, on our way for a brief chat with Ike, we warmed
to the old familiar view of a shapely headpiece to the valley—of Scope

End, leading to pyramidic Hindscarth and big brothers Dale Head (left) and Robinson (right). We were looking at a landscape cropped bare by sheep and ransacked by generations of quarrymen and by miners seeking copper, lead, some silver—and a lile bit of real gold. Or so "they" say. . .

Ike's farmyard is the place at which to admire the contrast between a neat and tidy dale, with its rich grazing land and floriferous meadows, and beyond the neat demarcation provided by walls—some tously fellsides, with a mini-jungle of bracken on the lower slopes.

Ike was in good form. His name is derived from Isaac. Everyone knows him as Ike. "Mebbe if things are not going well, I git worse names than that", he said.

He pointed out High Snab and said it was the only farm in the valley which belongs to the National Trust. We turned our heads to take in the majesty of some more high fells—Cat Bells, where your maiden aunt will not be out of breath on reaching the summit; also Maiden Moor and, of course, Hindscarth and Robinson, the humbling of which was that day's task.

Ike, who runs sheep on Robinson, told us it is not a particularly good "winter fell" and in worsening weather they drop down to the fell gate. Then, said Ike, "you've got to give them some hay and cake".

When driving sheep to or from the fell, the farmer and his son use an ancient lane and have three knowledgeable working dogs available in case the sheep get too frisky. The "gather" from Robinson takes four or five hours. As Ike says: "It depends on the day. On a nice cool day, it's easy".

He allowed me to pat his 13 year old dog. Ike smiled, then added: "You dog's like me—it's getten worse for wear".

Colin looked to see what Wainwright had written about Robinson. The note was somewhat apologetic. Poor old Robinson, despite his height of 2,417 ft, has been left with a plain appearance, especially when seen from Buttermere. Then it seems to be reclining languidly rather than standing to attention, like the big boys just across Buttermere.

I should imagine that Robinson looks best from a helicopter, flying in from the direction of Keswick when the shadows are lengthening.

Wainwright had at least done some meticulous drawings and he had done his homework, finding out a little more about the fell than its appearance. Perhaps he had a chat with his good friend Henry Marshall, the Kendal librarian, who had a splendid reference library.

The Robinson of the title was Richard Robinson, who became a major landowner in the reign of Henry VIII, when there was a good deal of monastic land going cheaply. Presumably because the monks had no special name for it, the dalesfolk would call it "Robinson's Fell" and, being sparing with words, had soon cut it down to—Robinson. Naming the fell should have been left to the Americans.

It could have been worse, said AW. The new owner of the estate might have been called Smith, Jones—or even Wainwright!

Mrs Linton (whose thoughts about Lakeland have been featured in quite a number of these notes about fells) was kind to Robinson. She called it "a grand old mountain" though it was "not one to take liberties with in misty weather or when the night is setting in. There have been sad adventures on Robinson, and aching hearts kept sore for long because of the dangerous ravines and the cleanly cut precipices belonging to him and veiled from the searching eye by night or cloud".

She mentioned the waterfall visible from the Hause, a force "where the broken crags are curiously uptorn, and where there is a punchbowl of glorious dimensions down below, and the figure of a huge bear, so they say, to be seen climbing upon the steepest part of the rock and dividing the water as it falls".

Victorian visitors on the Buttermere Round from Keswick had the summit of Robinson pointed out to them by the driver of their coach and four, which travelled "light" up steep hills—the healthier passengers having been requested to walk—and descended with a squealing that set everyone's teeth "on edge". What they heard was the sound of a primitive brake known as a "slipper" rubbing against the wheel.

When I sub-titled this piece about Robinson "Fools on the Moss". I was not thinking about us, though that title might have stuck. Nor had I in mind those who, approaching the summit from Buttermere, had to cross a glutinous tract of mossland.

The "fool" of the high mountains is the dotterel, a rare bird which once nested sparingly, and somewhat spasmodically, on some of the high, bare fells of Lakeland. It nests on the ground, of course, and records of early last century show that Robinson Fell was one of its breeding places.

This relatively small member of the plover family, with its broad eye stripes, grey throat and chestnut red upper breast, was under threat when Victorian collectors of bird skins and eggs dangled money in front of shepherds and encouraged them to collect any specimens they might find. A bird of the cloudy "tops" ended its life on display in musty rooms.

The dotterel has a partiality for big summit plateaux and fells with flattish spurs, which most certainly takes in the Buttermere country, though the Rhacomitrium heath which occurs at most of its remaining British nesting grounds is absent on Robinson.

The bird was considered to be a "fool" because it was so confiding. Sometimes, it might be stroked while incubating its eggs. It would make no attempt to run away. The hard-sitting dotterel was showing good sense, however. Stillness and his cryptic colouration ensured that it would not be easily seen by predators and to move from the eggs would be to run the risk of them becoming chilled by long exposure to wind or frost.

Thomas Heysham, one of the most diligent of dotterel-hunters in the first half of last century, spent five consecutive holidays in the Lake District before he "secured" a nest—on Robinson.

After visiting Ike, we left the car on a vacant patch of ground at the side of a byroad in the valley. The roads of Newlands have not yet outgrown their old status of country tracks and the motorist follows them as an act of faith rather than through a conviction that the destination will be reached.

We booted up, put the "mudflaps" into position to keep our lower legs warm as well as clean and were soon in a swinging pace, chattering away our cares or anxieties during the first half hour and then, in the spirit of Ruskin—who wrote "it is enough to be alive"— enjoying the sights, sounds and sensations of Lakeland.

We passed the white-washed church and its adjacent building which was the day school until 25 years ago. We headed for the cone-shaped Hindscarth but had time to admire the unpretentious but attractive 17th century farmsteads built of local stone, roofed with local slate and whitewashed so that they gleam amid the thousand shades of summer green.

We four clambered up the immense natural steps of Scope End, seeing traces of mining all around us, and reached the cairns of Hindscarth (at 2,385 ft) before being struck by thirst and hunger-pangs.

Stan reminded me of the time when, on opening my snack-box in a wooded part of Lakeland, I was attacked by a pheasant, had to beat it off with the box and had the anguish of seeing a Scots egg rolling down a steep bank into the beck.

Hindscarth has a name which is said to mean "pass of the deer". Perhaps the Lakeland reds were, in early times, driven to the cooking pot in the wee valley between Hindscarth and Robinson. Early Man knew how to manipulate the environment for his own ends and he hit the culinary jackpot if he succeeded in bringing down a red deer.

We saw some of Ike's sheep—mainly Swardles (Swaledales) though with a few of the bonnier but less valuable herdwicks. Ike says: "A herdwick's hardier than a Swaledale. You can mebbe keep more herdwicks. But the Swardle's worth a lot more".

It was on the high fells, between the daleheads, that shepherds and their stocks of sheep met. When strays were taken up during a "gather" a meet was organised so that they could be returned to their rightful owners. Shepherds' meets are still held but are now mainly social occasions, based on a pub.

Ike usually attends the meet held in November "against the Fish" at Buttermere. Many strays are now reported to their owners via the telephone and are collected by Land Rover and trailer.

How do they identify them? By the marks on their fleeces, horns and ears. Each flock has its own special marks. Those for Gill Brow are a red mark across the top of the back, a black "pop" and IW burnt on to the near horn.

Ear-clipping was another way of distinguishing sheep belonging to different owners. This was the old Norse "law mark", corrupted to "lug". In the old days, a naughty child was punished by having his/her "lugs rattled".

We left Hindscarth and worked our way round Little Dale to Robinson. On the long slog up Littledale Edge, I overtook a party from my home town. A middle-aged woman looked twice at me and we discovered we had been in the same school class at primary level!

On grassy Robinson, one or two parties arrived, shrugged their shoulders and went off to the rims of the plateau for better views. New arrivals from Buttermere had peat on their boots (and high up their legs) from the moss which gives Robinson a padded shoulder. One newcomer found terra firma where Robinson is crossed by two low outcrops of rock.

Having reached such a high elevation, little effort was needed to follow a spur eastwards to Dale Head (2,473 ft), where a special snack (left-overs and tepid tea) commemorated my 100th Wainwright.

We descended broken ground, on which walking was not easy, and used a path beside Great Gable, jnr., and a gill with the intriguing title of Fat Tongue. The map included industrial and farming terms— level (disused), workings, sheepfold and bield (shelter). In these parts, mining co-existed with sheep farming.

Dale Head was being mined as early as the 16th century. Castlenook (copper) Mines were opened at the turn of the 17th century by a man with the unCumbrian name of Daniel Hechstetter. The Climbing Hut shown on the map turned out to be substantial stone building.

Thence to the prosperous Goldthorpe mine, the Eldorado of Lakeland, which was being worked in the 13th century, though not under its present name, first used in the 16th century. Then the Goldthorpe mine was "the best in all England".

The Society for Mines Royal recruited German labour. Goldthorpe is derived from Gottes Gaab, or God's gift, and God certainly smiled on Newlands. One copper vein is said to have been nine feet thick. Re-opened in the mid-19th century, Goldthorpe yielded over three hundred tons of lead annually—for a few years.

We reached the vicinity of Low Snab at dusk. Scope End was silhouetted in the misty gloom. Lights were seen, high up, where some of the disused mine levels are to be found. It was unlikely that the light was being emitted by a giant species of glow-worm for it was at the head rather than the tail.

A human voice was heard. Five "glow-worms" formed a line-ahead formation for the descent of the fell. And so we had the magical sight of pin-pricks of light against the velvety mass of the fells as the day came to a typically calm and pleasant ending.

Mellbreak:
Not Quite A Mountain

NEARLY everything we had read about Mellbreak mentioned foxes and their hunters. The name of the fell (spelt with two l's) was adopted (with only one l) by the local pack of foxhounds. Those unfamiliar with Mellbreak Fell will doubtless have heard of the Melbreak Pack, one of six operating in Lakeland.

None of us has any special interest in fox-hunting, but Mellbreak beckoned, and not just because it was sanctified by Wainwright.

As we booted up in a parking space not far from the Kirkstile inn at Loweswater, Bob said the term should be "saddle up", for Mellbreak when viewed from the lake looks a bit like a saddle with two humps and a shallow depression in between.

We were in Stan's "backyard", for he was living at Eaglesfield. We envied him his close proximity to a hot bath when the day's walking was done.

Viewing Mellbreak from Kirkstile is to see the fell at its most majestic. Now, instead of a saddle, little else but the north top is in view and this huge natural pyramid blocks out half the sky.

Wainwright referred to Mellbreak as being isolated—aloof, indeed—its only allegiance being to cold, deep Crummock Water. Bob stressed this point. Mellbreak was not a Wainwright with ridges to link it with its neighbours. It demands an expedition of its own.

From the shore of Crummock Water side, this fell showed a craggy face, with loose material in which the foxes can den and ledges suitable for the twiggy, wool-lined nests of ravens. A pair begins building, or renovating an old nest as early as February and by late March or early April there might be nestlings to feed. Their hunger is met by the carcasses of sheep and lambs. The raven is a carrion-eater.

"Thoo'll 'appen know..." began a local man. And I guessed

correctly, judging by the embroidered fox-heads on his tie, that he was about to mention the Melbreak [one letter l]. He did.

I've chatted with t'auld end of Lakelanders who claimed that the fell foxes used to be larger, greyer, wilder and scarcer than the foxes of today. Before the blood of t'auld type became blended with that of foxes introduced last century, the fox was long in the leg, with a rough coat sprinkled with silvery hairs. It became known as the "greyhound" and was also known to be straight-necked [once disturbed, it didn't look back]. Chases of 50 and 60 miles were recorded.

The modern huntsman has a red jacket [hunting pink?] whereas the legendary John Peel—who hunted the Skiddaw country—had a coat so grey [hodden grey or undyed wool clipped from the backs of the herdwicks].

We had Mellbreak to ourselves. Only two other ramblers were seen when we were among the crags and dods on a roundabout way to tame Mellbreak, which is normally climbed by a direct route, up Raven Crag. That way, it is the rambler who is tamed.

Mellbreak—"little" Mellbreak, some call it, for it is only 1,676 ft high—is a decorative fell in relation to Crummock Water. Here is nature at her most artistic.

This mini-mountain of Mellbreak fills an important space splendidly, like a piece of stage scenery. Frank Carruthers has compared it to a headless sphinx, "with a fine curve of back and the shoulders a mere eight feet higher than the rump".

We could not image many people climbing Mellbreak unless they had the stimulus of bagging yet another Wainwright. The place must be peaceful for most of the time, which suits the foxes and the ravens in their glossy suits of undertaker-black.

We kept to the higher/drier slopes and managed to get across Mosedale without getting water in our boots. The hidden valley takes its name from the swampy nature of the terrain. In places, the ground is like a sponge, holding water and releasing it gently into the beck— or into the walker's boots.

Wainwright pointed out that Mosedale has only one tree, a holly, and he claimed that this was the only single tree to be honoured by the lone symbol of a tree on the Ordnance map.

Mellbreak is full of surprises. It has red "teeth", where pinnacles testify by their hue to the presence of iron in the rock. Yet it is not quite a mountain. It's a wonder that Mellbreak does not have an inferiority complex, with Whiteside, Grasmere and Whiteless Pike in view to the east of the lake.

Our expedition ended with a walk along the shore path. The wind was strengthening and the lake had white-tops, giving the impression of a sea held in captivity. In the cold depths of the lake are found char, a species of fish which became landlocked after the Ice Ages and adapted itself to fairly constricted freshwater locations.

Fishing for char is a skilful and distinctive operation, involving trolling from a boat with lines of great length and spinners made from bright objects, bits of metal cut to the required shape. An old friend used silver from the case of an old pocket watch.

The char, assuming a bright red belly, comes into shallow water at spawning time but is otherwise a creature of the chilly deeps.

When Bob mentioned char, he was thinking of his thermos flask. We drained it at the car, our heads tilting back not just to admit the liquid to our mouths but so that our eyes could take in the magnificence of Mellbreak's most imposing side.

Haystacks:
Wainwright's Last Peak

A LAKELAND granny used to tease her offspring when asked the whereabouts of someone. Avoiding the direct answer, granny would remark: "They're off milking the cows in haystacks". Or, more precisely, "Awa' milkin' t'coos in t'haystacks".

One of her grandsons told me he believed she had first heard this saying when, as a young lass, she worked in a farmhouse not far from Buttermere. (When grandfather was courting her, he travelled from Maryport to Buttermere, and back again, on a push-bike).

The grandson, a keen fell-walker, while trudging the Buttermere fells came across the remains of two stone buildings and recalled granny's remark. Was it here that the cows were milked while at their summer grazings? Or did Lanty Slee get into these parts to distil whisky? The distilling equipment was known as a "cow and worm", the cow being the kettle and the worm the coil condenser.

That is one story relating to Haystacks. Wainwright recorded the name as being Norse, meaning High Rocks, though he had heard the fanciful story that the fell was named because of the scattered tors on the summit resembling stacks of hay in a summer meadow.

Our group of four made a death-or-glory ascent straight up from the shores of Buttermere to High Crag and then descended to Haystacks.

The car was parked at Buttermere and, walking near the *Fish Hotel*, we crossed the valley towards Sour Milk Gill—the "sour milk" being tumbling water—then blundered in a conifered area before breaking out on to open ground and climbing into a vast corrie where we listened to the chacking of wheatears and the fluty voices of ring ouzels.

We left by a muscle-tightening ascent of what Wainwright called "Sheepbone Rake", with the croaky voices of ravens and a few minor

138

swear words from us making the air shiver.

At the head of the rake we followed a path to the summit of High Crag, joining what is to ramblers the equivalent of the motorist's M6—a broad and well-beaten way.

We glimpsed Ennerdale, lagged with the dark green of conifers, and descended an awesome scree on our way to Haystacks.

It was a busy summit. Innominate Tarn takes that name from being—nameless! (There was a suggestion, happily not adopted, that it be given the name Wainwright).

Stan took us to a perched boulder on a rock platform. The boulder was sketched by Wainwright, of course. He drew attention to the profile in shadow, of beaked nose, small mouth and prominent chin. He observed that some women have a face like that. Stan's name was Mother-in-law Rock!

We passed behind Green Crag into Dubs Quarry, with its old hut, and a storm came. We saw a family, the lady wearing a mini skirt and trying to control a golf umbrella in the swirling wind. Father limped behind holding the hand of a small child, who was limping, one leg being encased in plaster.

Our route was to the ridge above Honister Crag and on to the summit of Fleetwith Pike, which we now descended, painstakingly, over broken ground, to Buttermere and we stomped through the lakeside tunnel which was cut through living rock.

Haystacks can be handily climbed from Ennerdale Head, the footpath beginning near Black Sail Hut, a shepherds' bothy that was converted into a youth hostel in 1933. Wainwright was here during the filming by the BBC of his Coast to Coast Walk.

Black Sail has a most romantic setting. Having broken clear of the coniferous belt I saw the bumpy little peak of Haystacks in the respectable company of Green Gable, Great Gable (dominating the head of the valley), Kirk Fell and Pillar.

Black Sail, the small, single-storey "simple" grade hostel, more usually referred to as "hut", was acquired by the Forestry Commission as part of the old Gillerthwaite sheep farm, and the hut was leased to the YHA in 1932. It was adapted for use as a hostel through a donation of Professor Trevelyan in 1933.

Wainwright would feel at ease on his visit to Black Sail. He liked the simple life and did not like to see well-remembered places "modernised", as happened at Wasdale Head and various other places.

There's not much can go wrong with Black Sail. No electricity wires connect the place with the national grid. It runs on propane gas. The water comes off the fellside. A multi-purpose stove (wood or anthracite) heats the water, provides a background heat to the common room and enough heat to dry people's clothes on wet days. The hut has a resident cat—and no mice!

Black Sail is closed in winter. On its re-opening next spring, the place feels damp and chilly, but not for long. A former warden told me: "It's amazing, once you have got the fire lit, how quickly it comes right. Once you've got lots of hot water and have washed the place down, you can see the results of your efforts in the short term."

The common room is also the dining room and, in an emergency, an overflow dormitory. Boots lined the beams. Damp clothing was draped from a rack above the stove—such a rack of the type which AW would have seen at his childhood home in Blackburn. Operating with rope and pulleys, the rack normally hung just under the ceiling near the fire and was used for the airing of clothes.

I saw a cow horn, some antlers, guitar, books, a photograph of Harry Chapman, who was secretary of the Lakeland Region for many years, and some prints of Black Sail in its original state.

The warden's room is tiny, while being an improvement on that of the original warden. He slept by the fire in the common room. The hut was extended at the back to provide a capacious kitchen.

Black Sail hut looks best in the evening light. In Ennerdale, which faces west, the sun goes down over the lake and lights up the whole of the north-east side of Gable Crag. The hut's setting has much to do with its charm and popularity. Almost everybody in hostelling has heard of Black Sail. One satisfied hosteller wrote in the visitors' book:

> Why, o why, do we do it?
> Sit in front of the fire at Black Sail
> and you have the answer.

To climb Haystacks from Ennerdale is often a pleasanter experience than from Buttermere, when the fell is invariably in shade. Haystacks failed to qualify for inclusion in Wainwright's list of the best half dozen fells only because of its inferior height. Another thousand feet would have made all the difference.

Yet this was his favourite mountain. Here he loved to walk, remarking that he might wander on Haystacks for hour after hour and he would always find something different to look at, such as small crags and sinuous paths.

Here, on his last visit, with a BBC camera crew, the heavens wept and he was chilled and soaked. They portrayed AW, solitary but not lonely, sitting on a rain-swept hillside, his head bowed in deep thought.

He told Eric Robson, his companion in many television programmes, that "I shall end up here". Someone would carry him up in a small box and leave him on the fell. Yet he would not lack company. Several keen fell-walkers had written to tell him that they had chosen Haystacks as their last resting place.

When AW died, his ashes were deposited near Innominate Tarn.

The Little Rowan Tree:

A Sort Of Monument

ON AN unforgettable day in 1980, my post included an article and two photographs from AW.

Twenty years before, he was toiling up the steep trackless gully of Hassnesshow Beck from Buttermere, pioneering a route to the summit of Robinson, when he noticed what appeared to be two twigs sticking upright from a low crag at the side of the ravine.

"Curious, I climbed up to inspect, and found to my surprise that the twigs were in fact the branches of a tiny rowan that had secured a root-hold in a thin crack in the rock face, the seed having evidently blown there or been dropped by a passing bird.

"With no visible means of sustenance, and no root run, it had nevertheless secured a firm hold. Rowans, of course, are tenacious little beggars in infancy, yet I had to admire the courage and determination of this puny specimen, surviving against all the odds. It seemed to have a message for me. Don't quit. Don't give up. Keep trying".

Wainwright could not forget his little rowan tree. "The lesson it had for me helped me on the rest of the climb. When later I described the route in the book I was writing I mentioned it, the following being an extract from the page . . ."

And there it was, to the right of Goat Fell—a note about the young rowan. "Can it survive?" asked AW. "Will some kind reader write to the author in 1970 and say it is still alive and well?"

A year or two went by, and letters began to arrive, all assuring Wainwright that the rowan was still alive and flourishing. "Since then, I have had a great many reports about the state of the tree, and even a poem, from readers all over the country, and from their accompanying photographs I have watched it grow in stature over the past 20 years."

142

In 1970, ten years on, he received a sheaf of correspondence. A party from Whitehaven wrote a saga of their visit, illustrated by camera studies and graphic drawings.

Now Wainwright was updating me. "On New Year's Day, 1980, the Whitehaven party made another pilgrimage, braving the snow and ice, to confirm its continuing survival, and again supplied photographs and more dramatic pen-and-ink illustrations of their arduous assent".

No single feature he had mentioned in his books had brought him more letters, "not even Jack's Rake", and they had given him great pleasure. "The rowan isn't my tree, but I have developed a proprietary interest in it and think of it as mine. It will outlive me and carry my name as a sort of monument. I could not wish for a better".

Epilogue

WAINWRIGHT said: "I was always concerned more with the mountains than the valleys". In his early days in Lakeland, the district had charm, a delicate quality which went with new roads, increased traffic and the hub-hub of mass tourism.

He loved the sense of freedom which fell-walking gave him. In his apprenticeship days, he might walk from dawn to dusk and not see another human being, except perhaps a fell farmer, dog at heel, attending to his stock of herdwick sheep.

He rejoiced that the felltops had changed little, if at all, in the half century he knew them, and he celebrated his love for the fells in over 40 books. He wrote and drew incessantly with a consistently high quality. His books are his principal memorial.

Wainwright, among the most private of men, shared his love of the fells with a vast reading public. When he began to compile his guides, at the rate of one hand-written page a day, and with only £35 in the bank, he little knew that before his eyesight failed he would produce the longest love-letter ever written.

Towards the end of his life, he bowed to the pressure of Media attention, granting interviews and allowing the BBC to make documentaries based on his books. They attracted an audience numbered in millions.

So we have preserved for our delectation his thoughts, his art, his appearance and manner. Those of us fortunate enough to have known him are conscious that he transformed our way of looking at the fell country and, by encouraging us to get up and walk—to get to the top!—he prolonged our active lives.